W9-DEV-920

GROUNDWORK GUIDES

Series Editor
Jane Springer

GROUNDWORK GUIDES

Cities
John Lorinc

Groundwood Books
House of Anansi Press

Toronto Berkeley

Groundwood Books / House of Anansi Press
110 Spadina Avenue, Suite 801, Toronto, Ontario M5V 2K4
or c/o Publishers Group West
1700 Fourth Street, Berkeley, CA 94710

We acknowledge for their financial support of our publishing
program the Canada Council for the Arts, the Government of Canada
through the Book Publishing Industry Development Program (BPIDP)
and the Ontario Arts Council.

 ONTARIO ARTS COUNCIL
CONSEIL DES ARTS DE L'ONTARIO

Library and Archives Canada Cataloguing in Publication
Lorinc, John
Cities : a Groundwork guide / John Lorinc.
Includes bibliographical references and index.
ISBN-13: 978-0-88899-820-0 (bound).
ISBN-10: 0-88899-820-1 (bound).
ISBN-13: 978-0-88899-819-4 (pbk.)
ISBN-10: 0-88899-819-8 (pbk.)
1. Cities and towns. 2. Rural-urban migration. 3. Urbanization.
I. Title.
HT151.L675 2008   307.76   C2007-9005214-X

Design by Michael Solomon
Printed and bound in Canada

Contents

For my mother, Eva, and my sister, Julie

Chapter 1
The Urban Century

The year 2008 marked a watershed moment in the evolution of human society. For the first time in history, more than half of the world's 6.6 billion inhabitants were living in cities rather than rural areas. In the industrialized world, the population has become steadily more urbanized since the mid-nineteenth century, when the Industrial Revolution transformed villages and market towns into manufacturing and commercial centers. By the late twentieth century, however, many countries in the developing world — especially in Asia, Latin America and the Middle East — were experiencing extremely rapid urbanization as millions of people were leaving, or fleeing, the countryside to find jobs and a new life in big cities.[1]

There's no reason to expect this trend to slow or reverse itself, so the health of cities is a topic of enormous significance. After all, if most of us live in cities, we need to understand how these complex places function — socially, economically, culturally, spiritually, environmentally and politically. We must be conscious of how cities throughout history prospered or fell into decline, why some became dynamic hubs of cultural or scientific innovation while others allowed tyrants to build brutal regimes. In an age of mass migration and global trade, we should also be aware of the experiences of cities like New York,

Hong Kong, Toronto — places that have been rapidly reshaped by international commerce and immigrants with new cultural tastes, architectural practices and commercial connections.

Yet as much as we need to be aware of the many strands of urban history, the extraordinary challenges facing twenty-first-century cities have no precedent. The past offers few lessons on how megacities with tens of millions of residents — many of them desperately poor — should manage growth, deliver services or govern themselves. In some of the richest Western cities, such as Los Angeles and London, staggering wealth co-exists with grinding poverty. In cities like São Paulo and Istanbul, dense shanty towns have sprung up on hillsides and marginal land. Globalization has created explosive economic growth in urban China while sapping the vitality of once-prosperous cities in the US "rust belt." Around the world, urban population growth and consumerism are contributing to extreme forms of environmental degradation: sprawl, pollution, global warming due to greenhouse gas emissions, water contamination, overconsumption of nonrenewable energy sources, mountains of waste.

No one disputes the seriousness of these problems. At the same time, there is room for optimism. Throughout history, urban centers have often proven to be not only highly adaptable, but engines of civilization and oases of tolerance. Cities have been described as the greatest of all human creations.[2] Their task, in this century, will be nothing less than saving humanity from its worst excesses.

According to the *Oxford English Dictionary*, "city" derives from a twelfth-century Middle English word coined to describe human settlements that were larger — and more important — than towns. These were religious centers, commercial capitals or walled cities built for strategic purposes.

The emergence of a word is always an important signpost. It acknowledges a society's need to name something new. There had been great cities long before the twelfth century, of course — ancient Babylon, Athens, Alexandria, Imperial Rome, Kyoto. But after the collapse of the Roman Empire, many European and Middle Eastern cities fell into a long period of decline that lasted until the eleventh and twelfth centuries, when urban centers began to re-assert their importance.

What, then, *is* a city if not just a large town? This question raises others: how far does a city's influence extend? Who should govern its residents? What are the rights and obligations of those who live in and near cities? And how do local politics shape urban areas?

Begin with the problem of boundaries. Medieval cities often surrounded themselves with formidable walls to keep out invaders. But these cities expanded as traders and refugees settled outside the walls. Other cities, such as London, emerged as clusters of towns blending into one another, creating highly integrated urban areas with diverse economies that attracted newcomers from surrounding rural regions.

To this day, big cities grow relentlessly, expanding into the hinterland beyond their fringes. In the West, this phenomenon is known as "sprawl" — the outward push of subdivisions, shopping malls, highways and industrial parks. In the developing world, meanwhile, many major cities are ringed by vast slums (a.k.a. squatter communities or shanty towns, or in Brazil, *favelas)* that grow on steep slopes or derelict government land.

Such development patterns always create tensions in the relationships between the urban core and its periphery. Economically, the influence of cities tends to radiate outward, even though wealth flows into urban regions. In North

America, major metropolitan areas are surrounded by "exurbs" — quiet towns that may appear to have a rural character, but whose residents commute to the city or depend on its presence in other ways. In commercial hubs like Tokyo or Frankfurt, the urban influence extends even further: those who work in the financial districts of such cities routinely make investment decisions with global implications.

The wealth generated by large cities causes them to physically expand as they attract economic migrants and those forced off their farms. Such metropolitan areas, in turn, become increasingly interconnected settlements. City-dwellers (even those living in shanty towns) don't restrict themselves to just one small part of an urban area. They may live and socialize in one neighborhood but work in another. Businesses function locally, regionally and perhaps even internationally. Travelers and newcomers are constantly coming and going.

Such activity requires urban infrastructure. Cities depend on public works — ports, roads, sewers, fresh water. Waste needs to be removed to prevent the outbreak of disease. There must be some means of providing security and protecting public health, as well as systems for regulating the interplay between public and private spaces.

These tasks traditionally fall to some form of local government that collects taxes from urban dwellers and invests these funds in public amenities and services within the borders of the city. The nature of those governments varies greatly: many ancient cities were established and ruled by emperors. In more recent times, cities have been governed by merchants and elected representatives. But in all cases, the outward push of cities posed a conundrum: as the geographical reach and the urban population grew, how did local government adapt itself to the ever-changing shape and composition of the urban area?

In ancient Greece, a city and the surrounding region was described as a "city-state," an autonomous political entity known as a *polis*. Today, sprawling city-regions are managed by numerous municipal agencies and local government bodies. In some countries, like Spain and Japan, the very largest urban clusters have regional governments with a mandate to manage issues — such as transportation and air quality — that cut across municipal boundaries and straddle the urban-suburban divide.

The challenge of managing a populous urban area is formidable, and has, through the ages, led to great achievements in engineering, architecture, culture, even medicine. Roman engineers designed sophisticated aqueducts, roads and sewers to meet the needs of a sprawling, imperial capital. More than two millennia later, municipal officials in Victorian-era Toronto established sanitation systems to combat child mortality.

But the history of cities suggests that ambitious urban rulers often want to do more than deliver public services efficiently. Some cities have been preoccupied by erecting major religious institutions, while others sponsored the construction of magnificent cultural or political structures. Many cities focused on the commercial needs of merchants and guilds. Capital cities swept away slums to make way for stately boulevards or political institutions.

Social justice has also been a preoccupation of local government. In the nineteenth century, reformers in North America and Great Britain persuaded municipalities to build parks, recreation facilities, schools, housing for the poor and public libraries to provide the urban working classes with a respite from crowded tenements and factories.

During the last century, the mission of local government expanded even further. In New York City, between the 1940s and 1960s, city officials undertook what was almost a wholesale redesign of Gotham, building vast social housing complexes, enormous recreation areas, networks of highways and bridges, and cultural institutions.

In Tokyo during the early 1980s, the national government took the lead in promoting urban change to establish the city, known until 1868 as Edo, as a global center of commerce. In partnership with regional authorities and large multinational corporations, state officials oversaw the development of huge amounts of new downtown office space in the city's core, a process that involved the displacement of small older businesses and residential neighborhoods.[3]

Not all of these undertakings are successful or even well-intentioned. But the compulsion to improve the city — to impose order on what may seem like chaos and crowding — is a hallmark of local government.

This is not a new impulse. The Greek philosopher Aristotle regarded the city as an extension of the household, as well as a "partnership" that emerged organically from the political instincts of human beings. In his view, the raison d'etre of the city, and its own form of government, was to foster "the good life." "While coming into being for the sake of living," he wrote, "[the city] exists for the sake of living well."[4]

Almost 2,500 years later, we still debate what it means to "live well" within the context of the city, and how cities should manage themselves to ensure their citizens may attain this goal. Does living well mean being able to choose a suburban lifestyle that provides the conveniences of the city without the crowding of its core? Or does living well suggest a social justice agenda that raises the standard of living of the poorest urban dwellers? Perhaps living well entails the spiritual, cultural and intellectual improvement of the citizens of the city. In an era of massive urban regions, the goal of living well also encompasses an environmental agenda that seeks to improve urban air quality and reduce car use. Today, when local politicians and big city mayors make speeches about improving urban "quality of life," they are unconsciously invoking Artistotle.

Of course, in most cities, quality of life remains an elusive goal for many residents. Poverty, extremely polluted air, the high cost of living, a shortage of decent housing, the stresses of long commutes — the list of problems that detracts from urban quality of life is extensive. Nor is it new. During the 1840s, the philosopher Friedrich Engels wandered through the appalling slums of industrial Manchester and the experience informed his writings about the struggles of the British working class. Since the Renaissance, in fact, urban planners, social reformers, architects and artists have been moved to design "ideal cities" and utopian communities in order to correct the injustices and spiritual impoverishment associated with city living.[5]

In considering the meaning of phrases like "the good life" and "quality of life," we must also remember to ask, "whose life?" Modern municipalities tackle this question all the time: how should they plan and spend tax dollars in order to achieve the broadest benefit for their inhabitants? Urban history is littered with examples of how local governments achieved just the opposite, either intentionally or accidentally — inner-city highways that uprooted working-class neighborhoods, ostensibly progressive public housing projects that were actually meant to isolate racial minorities from the mainstream, costly infrastructure projects that turned out to be fiascos.

Local governments are constantly making subtle and not-so-subtle distinctions between residents, and deciding which groups are more or less entitled to the city's support. Interestingly, the Latin origin of "city" is *civitas*, which refers to the condition of citizenship within a self-governing community. In other words, long before the emergence of the modern nation-state, the ancient Greeks recognized the link between city living and the political rights associated with citizenship. But they also knew that not everyone who lived in the city enjoyed the full benefits of urban citizenship. There were slaves. And women couldn't participate in Athenian direct democracy in the fourth and fifth centuries BC.

Over the centuries, cities have continued to tolerate the presence of second-class citizens. Many European cities, beginning with Venice, had ghettos — often walled areas established by municipal governments and reserved exclusively for Jews, who lacked civil rights. In many American cities, from the Civil War until the 1960s, African Americans were limited to specified neighborhoods or excluded from others. Instead of walls, cities used legal instruments, such as zoning rules or restrictive covenants.

In the megacities of the developing world, we see a much more entrenched variation on the theme of two-tier urban citizenship. Shanty towns, populated by millions of desperately poor people who have flocked to the big cities looking for work, are routinely denied access to basic municipal services, even though these communities occupy land within the urban region and represent a large portion of the urban population. Meanwhile, affluent residents often live in heavily guarded compounds or "green zones" policed by private security forces.

Even in relatively affluent industrialized cities, there are evident distinctions. Housing for refugees, migrant laborers and the poor is often located in isolated areas, such as the *banlieue* of suburban Paris. Many municipalities raise funds by taxing property owners and then favoring their needs above others. The result is that those who don't own real estate — tenants, students, recent immigrants, low-income families — have less say in determining the affairs of the city. In some cities, low voter turnout among these groups further entrenches their disenfranchisement. The good life continues to elude many city-dwellers.

No nation has ever solved the most intractable dilemmas of human existence. Poverty, injustice, violence, unequal access to resources — every society is destined to grapple, in its own way and with greatly varying degrees of success, with these fundamental problems. Regional, national and supranational governments today devote enormous amounts of time and energy to tackling issues such as poverty, regional development, AIDS, trade, security and the environment.

Due to global population trends and mass urbanization, it is increasingly at the level of the city that such challenges are experienced most acutely. But this demographic reality may offer cause for guarded optimism. There's no doubt that too much proximity, coupled with poverty or war, creates highly combustible social tensions. Yet the intensity of city living can also give rise to empathy, innovation and collective action. By virtue of their size, large cities instinctively generate wealth, and thus provide the possibility of an improved standard of living for their inhabitants.

The city, as Aristotle said, is the natural stage for our innate political inclinations and our highest aspirations. It was true in 300 BC, and it is just as true in 2008.

Chapter 2
Urban Forms and Functions

In AD 808, Charlemagne, the leader of the Holy Roman Empire, ordered that a castle be built on a rocky outcropping at the confluence of the Alster and Elbe rivers in what is now northern Germany. Its purpose was strategic: to defend against invading Slavs from the east. But the castle soon evolved into a fortress town named Hamburg, which was to become a religious center and then a free imperial port with prized access to merchant shipping lanes in the North Sea and beyond. Today, Hamburg is a thriving city-state of almost 2 million people, Germany's second-largest metropolitan region.

Almost all cities begin modestly. Sometimes, the location is determined by key geographical features: harbors, strategic heights of land, oases, even mountaintops. The ancient cities were founded on the muddy flats around the Tigris and Euphrates rivers. Toronto began as a tiny colonial settlement on the edge of a swamp near a lake.

While historians long believed that cities originated in Mesopotamia in the fourth millennium BC and then spread elsewhere, archeologists have identified even earlier urban settlements in Africa, Latin America and the Far East. "[T]he so-called urban revolution flared independently in several places on earth at different times," writes architectural historian Spiro Kostof.[1]

There are competing theories about why cities emerge where they do. Some historians and economists argue that they took root in places where people came to trade surplus food and goods. Others point to cities that grew out of military fortifications or sacred places sanctioned by various deities. Yet a castle or a temple may have been built to serve a pre-existing settlement. So the question is, which came first? Kostof argues that although it's difficult to pinpoint a precise cause behind the establishment of an urban settlement, cities do not emerge organically but as a result of human intention and political power:

> [N]o city, however arbitrary its form may appear to us, can be said to be "unplanned." Beneath the strangest twist of lane or alley, behind the most fitfully bounded public place, lies an order beholden to prior occupation, to the features of the land, to long-established conventions of the social contract, to a string of compromises between individual rights and the common will.[2]

Cities, moreover, are often planned, constructed and rebuilt in distinctive patterns that reflect prevailing political or economic priorities, religious beliefs and the local topography. Some cities were initially laid out according to a geometrical grid with streets and major blocks. Others utilized a radial shape, with streets emanating from a central point.

Many cities adapt their physical form to the natural environment, with development following the ridge of a hill or the slope of a mountain. Meandering rivers or ravine systems interrupt a street grid, while other land forms — for example, a desert — create natural boundaries. Yet cities are also built in defiance of the geography. Port cities like Hong Kong and New York grew upwards in response to space constraints. Venice was built on lagoon islands by refugees fleeing the chaos that accompanied the decline of the Roman Empire. The location initially provided security, but Venice's inhabitants later learned to exploit their city's unique configuration to promote sea trade and establish their political independence.

As cities grow and age, their form becomes increasingly complicated. This evolution often arises from economic development and population growth, as well as political independence. Throughout Europe in the Middle Ages, some settlements, such as Hamburg after 1189, came to be known as "free" cities, with their own charters. These cities were able to divorce themselves from feudal land-ownership structures, develop trade relationships with other cities, and offer peasants a chance to win their freedom.

In the relatively young cities of North America, older downtown areas with rundown low-rise structures have been redeveloped with high-rise office and apartment towers while planning on the suburban fringe is typically driven by developers and cars.

Urban forms also evolve due to changing political systems and spiritual mores. In some Middle Eastern centers that trace back to the Roman Empire, classical urban forms gave way to dense souks with narrow alleys as those cities became increasingly Islamic. The reason: Islamic law attached greater importance to private property and domestic privacy than to publicly administered civic spaces.[3]

Yet throughout history, countless cities have been physically altered in much more drastic ways, thanks to fires, wars,

What Is a City?

Lewis Mumford describes the city as a "point of maximum concentration for the power and culture of a community." "The city," he wrote in 1961, "broke down the parsimonious self-sufficiency and dreary narcissism of village culture."[4] In his study of urban form through history, *The City Shaped*, Spiro Kostof elaborates on this definition with his own list of features:

1. Density. Cities are not only populous, they are concentrated and "energized."
2. "Cities come in clusters." They are surrounded by towns and villages.
3. There is some kind of physical, social or political boundary.
4. Differentiation. Cities have rich and poor residents, many specialized occupations, ethnic groups, religions, castes.
5. A city is linked to key sources of income, from trade, natural resources, political patronage.
6. The city relies on written records, such as laws and property titles.
7. There is an interdependence between the city and the surrounding countryside.
8. Cities are defined by monumental structures, like temples, aqueducts, cultural buildings, office towers and political institutions.
9. Ultimately, "cities are made up of buildings and people."[5]

invasions and the agendas of new regimes intent on erasing the artifacts of the past and rebuilding in ways that correspond to their own aims and ideologies. The early popes, eager to assert their authority, dismantled much of pagan Rome. In our age, China's Communist regime tore down the monumental walls surrounding Beijing's Forbidden City in order to build arterial roads and apartment blocks. In some such cases, the goal isn't subtle: "In Mexico City," says heritage expert Anthony Tung, "the heritage of the Aztecs was purposely obliterated as part of a plan to subjugate a conquered people."[6]

Prior to the Spanish conquest, Mexico City was known as Tenochtitlán, a magisterial metropolis with more inhabitants than any city in Spain in the sixteenth century.[7] Built in a valley with lakes and a sophisticated irrigation system, Tenochtitlán dazzled Spanish conquistadors with its watery network of canals and bridges, as well as the pyramid-shaped temples, palaces and fortified walls anchored to the lake bottom.[8]

That Tenochtitlán had such a core illustrates another hallmark of urban form. Cities throughout history have tended to organize themselves around one or more focal points, districts where that community's most valued structures, monuments and institutions are situated. In Greek cities, writes Tung, "[t]he agora was a public square and marketplace and the central location for many of the collective activities of Athens.... In classical Athens, the agora gradually became the lower city's largest and most formal plaza, framed by many of the most important buildings of civic life."[9] Other examples include temples, palaces, cathedrals, minarets, citadels, cultural venues, seats of government, arenas, factories, train stations, hotels, radio towers, and the office towers that make up the skyline of our era. Some urban writers, in fact, use the word "citadel" to describe the steel-and-glass forests that typify the heart of many modern cities.

The compulsion to create an urban core seems to be hardwired into the way we build cities. In some urban settlements, the existence of two or more core areas reveals intra-urban rivalries — between commercial and political interests, or among rival business factions. Large modern cities like Los Angeles are made up of a network of core and sub-core zones. Their existence may indicate political rivalries between adjacent municipalities within a single metropolitan region, or between cliques of developers, major landlords and corporate head offices. The primary core, however, serves to consolidate urban power, which is symbolized by the concentration of a city's highest architectural achievements.

In the same way, the absence of a core, or its long-term decline, is evidence of urban instability. Beginning in the 1960s, many cities in the US, Canada and Europe saw the population of their downtowns begin to fall as the inner-city residents moved to newer, and often safer, suburbs, while businesses and employers relocated out of older industrial/commercial districts. For some cities, this trend began to reverse itself by the 1980s. In Detroit, the downtown died because of racial strife and economic restructuring in the car industry. These hollowed-out cities don't recover easily. Indeed, it is not a coincidence that the world's most dynamic cities also have thriving, populous cores.

As we've seen, cities have complex origins and their growth shifts dramatically over time. Once they reach a critical mass, most cities come to resemble highly interdependent ecosystems. But throughout history, many cities evolved — either by happenstance or through acts of political will — into places strongly associated with specific roles.

Sacred Cities
In the 1840s, Joseph Smith and Brigham Young, leaders of the Church of Jesus Christ of Latter Day Saints, laid out plans for a new city that could serve as a US site for the Second Coming. Salt Lake City, Utah, nestled on a sprawling plain beneath majestic mountains, became the spiritual center for the world's Mormons. It is arguably the youngest of the world's sacred cities, many of which date back to the dawn of the urban age

and can be found throughout Asia, the Middle East and Latin America.

Lewis Mumford, the noted urban critic, points out that humans first congregated in order to pray or make sacrifices. That habit led to the construction of the earliest shrines, and then the settlements that grew up around them. Citing examples such as the grand Mayan temples located in present-day Peru, urban historian Joel Kotkin points out that "religious structures — temples, cathedrals, mosques, and pyramids— have long dominated the landscape and imagination of great cities."[10]

Sacred cities sometimes sprang up around a place of pilgrimage (e.g., Lourdes, in France). Others, like Vatican City (inside Rome), functioned as a religion's spiritual and administrative headquarters. Three of the world's great faiths — Judaism, Islam and Christianity— trace their origins to a handful of Middle Eastern cities.

Mecca, located in modern-day Saudi Arabia, was the birthplace of Muhammad (born in AD 570) and continues to function as the end point of a mass annual pilgrimage for Muslims from all over the world. The city remains off-limits to non-Muslims.

Such dictums reveal how sacred cities have been highly divided spaces. Conquering regimes loot and destroy religious structures. New regimes may also alter existing temples to reflect their beliefs. Early Christians built the Hagia Sophia in Constantinople in the third century AD. A thousand years later, the Turks transformed it into a mosque.

Of all sacred cities, Jerusalem may well be the most disputed, the target of the medieval Crusader armies that swept across Europe, forcibly converting Jews and other heathens. The city of King David, the Temple Mount and the so-called

Wailing Wall, Jerusalem is sacred to Jews. Yet the old city also contains the Via Della Rosa and the Church of the Holy Sepulcher, places of enormous significance to Christians. Meanwhile, the Dome of the Rock mosque is located atop the ruins of the temple. It was built at the place where the prophet Muhammad was said to have ascended to heaven.

Jerusalem is currently the political capital of the State of Israel, but Palestinians have long demanded that the city be partitioned to reflect their historic presence there. That Jerusalem has been a flash point in the long-running Israeli-Palestinian conflict vividly illustrates the enormous spiritual significance invested in sacred cities.

Political Cities

Between 1956 and 1960, Brazil constructed a new federal capital to replace Rio de Janeiro. Located in a tropical interior region, Brasília is one of the world's only purpose-built political capitals, created using the stark, geometrical designs of post-war Modernism. At the heart of Brasília lies a grand 200-meter-wide (656-feet-wide) axis, abutted by austere office buildings housing key government ministries, the congress, the supreme court, the president's office and the city's cathedral.

Since the dawn of the age of the nation-state, political cities emerged as symbolic urban centers whose form reflected their ambitions. Cities like Washington, DC, New Delhi and Ottawa are dominated by formalized districts set aside for government buildings. Planned in the 1790s by Pierre L'Enfant, Washington, DC, is a city of grand baroque avenues radiating out of traffic circles. The city is focused on the Mall, a ceremonial green space surrounded by classical government buildings, with the looming US Congress at the east end.

Even poor nations invest substantial resources in their political capitals. In the early 1960s, the eccentric, brilliant American architect Louis Kahn was commissioned to design an iconic legislative building in Dacca, a monument to the newly independent state of Bangladesh.

Political cities are dominated by government activities and the extensive white-collar workforce associated with bureaucracies, legislatures and the judiciary. The downtown office buildings are crowded with lobbyists, nongovernmental organizations, diplomats and media outlets. These cities often have comfortable neighborhoods or enclaves for bureaucrats, as well as a cosmopolitan ambience. Another feature of political cities is that they tend to have a concentration of national cultural institutions.

Athens, during its Golden Age (500-400 BC), was the prototype of the political city. Presiding over a *polis* known as Attica, the citizens of Athens (male property owners) maintained a democratic system of self-government. The city's revenues were invested in public works, civic spaces and monumental temples like the Parthenon.[11]

The modern political city, by contrast, tends to have a more impaired ability to govern itself. Local government institutions are typically subservient to national governments, which own vast tracts of urban land and can impose their own agendas on the city. Such cities can also be places with stark divisions. Washington, DC, is a racially and economically polarized city, with some of the poorest neighborhoods in the US. Not coincidentally, the Congress retains direct authority over the District of Columbia, meaning its residents have no elected officials in the Senate or the House of Representatives.

Imperial Cities

At various times in history, certain cities have emerged as the command centers of far-flung military empires — Imperial Rome, Constantinople during Byzantium, London in the eighteenth and nineteenth centuries, when the British Empire extended around the world.

Rome, according to legend, was founded in 753 BC by brothers Remus and Romulus, who'd been abandoned beside the Tiber River and then raised by a wolf. It would take several hundred years before Rome reached its peak as a city of a million during the first century AD, presiding over an extensive empire with 50 million inhabitants.[12] Anthony Tung says that Rome, during this period, maintained an extraordinary inventory of public buildings, such as palaces, temples, amphitheaters, pools, baths, arches and administrative buildings.[13] The city also built an extensive network of aqueducts, roads and sewers to support the needs of its huge population.

Even more than political cities, imperial cities reveal the grandiose ambitions of their rulers. From the 1400s onward, the heart of Beijing was the Forbidden City, a grand walled precinct of concentric rectangles reserved for the Ming emperor and his mandarins.[14] The walls, Tung says, "established the harmonious geometric alignment of the capital with the poles of the Chinese cosmos. Their size and extent proclaimed the authority of the emperor and the kingdom. [And] they symbolized the orderliness of Chinese society, in which every inhabitant's house, courtyard, and daily life…was also aligned with the giant grid of the capital city and the earth."[15]

Monumental civic trappings don't come cheap. The Roman emperors and senators ordered the empire's relentless expansion in part to "secure the resources to sustain the city's swelling numbers of households, no matter what the cost in human lives," notes historian Joel Kotkin.[16] Rome extended citizenship to those in the conquered lands and established outposts on the frontiers that the Romans transformed into formal settlements which would grow into cities such as London, Budapest and Alexandria. During the eras of the Ottoman and British empires, Istanbul and London also functioned as the political and commercial command centers of networks of colonial cities and resource-rich territories.

Such empires have tended to collapse slowly but inexorably. Their size rendered them administratively unmanageable, but decline also occurred due to the mounting decadence and greed of the ruling classes that dominated the capitals.

Colonial Cities

The northern Indian city of Delhi is one of the world's oldest urban regions, serving for several centuries as the political and commercial capital for the Mughal empire. In 1911, the British rulers moved their Indian capital from Calcutta to Delhi. Swaths of ancient Delhi were torn down to make way for a sprawling administrative district designed by architect Edward Lutyens. Configured around majestic axes and imposing government buildings on a plan inspired by Washington, DC, New Delhi became an urban symbol of the British Raj.

Outwardly expanding empires have long marked their territories by creating urban outposts and satellites, cities that contain the architectural, political and cultural imprimatur of these political powerhouses. Ancient cities, such as Ephesus in western Turkey, bear the architectural legacy of various Greek and Roman rulers. Between the seventeenth and nineteenth centuries, the dominant European powers — France, Spain,

Portugal and Britain — built colonial cities throughout the Americas, Africa and Asia.

In Old Montreal, important religious and administrative buildings were designed to evoke the grandeur of Paris and the administrative reach of France. Havana, founded in 1515 by Spanish conquistadors, began as a fortification and later functioned as a major port for the thriving sugar and spice trade in the Caribbean. Evoking the style of Spanish cities like Seville and Granada, Old Havana's layout and architecture show the influence of the colonialists, although the city would later come to be dominated by other imperial powers — first the British, in the nineteenth century, and then the Soviet Union, in the twentieth.

Merchant Cities

At the dawn of the seventeenth century, in the wake of a war between Holland and Spain, the newly independent city of Amsterdam emerged as one of the world's first great merchant cities. It was, says Kotkin, "a dense modern city noteworthy not so much for its heroic statues and great boulevards, churches or palaces as for its teeming alleys, bustling wharves and clean and comfortable residences."[17] With a religiously diverse population and a large contingent of skilled craftspeople, Amsterdam became the hub of a global trading empire. Dutch firms produced high-value export goods like dyes, linen and furniture, while its engineers and scientists worked throughout Europe and the Americas.[18] It was an urban empire built not on military might, but on commercial relationships, tolerance and innovation.

In today's age of globalized trade, many of the world's wealthiest cities are centers of commerce and finance. Though

Urban Markets

Markets are a fixture of cities — those zones where merchants and their customers meet to trade not just goods but also gossip, cultural traditions and business contacts. Throughout history, cities have created purpose-built public spaces and buildings to function as markets and trade centers. Some are municipally run, while others are owned cooperatively by merchants' associations or private companies, as is the case with contemporary shopping malls and big-box stores.

But urban retail activity typically spills out of such places and into streets that become market districts, such as the teeming *qasaba* in medieval Cairo. Local growers and merchants set up stalls and sell their wares or produce. In Toronto, Kensington Market is a lively warren of narrow streets lined by merchants' stalls, bakeries and restaurants. Established by Eastern European Jews who settled in the city in the 1910s, Kensington is constantly being reshaped by immigrants from Europe, Asia and Latin America.

Specialization and concentration is another hallmark of urban markets. In present-day cities, certain retail areas come to be known for a certain category of good — clothing, antiques, specialty foods, books. There's a block near the theater district off Times Square, in New York, where almost all the shops sell musical instruments. The so-called Diamond District is a few blocks uptown. Great commercial cities also operate cavernous trade/convention centers, as well as wholesale produce markets, such as Tokyo's vast fish market, where sushi suppliers service customers around the world.

What's interesting is how enduring these business habits are. Booksellers and publishers began gathering for an annual trade fair in Frankfurt over 500 years ago — a tradition that persists to this day. The Grand Bazaar in Istanbul, which is more than 600 years old, has meandering corridors specializing in spices, rugs, jewelry and fabrics. The physical concentration of choice and competition creates a critical mass that benefits both buyer and seller. The modern-day shopping center may be a sanitized descendant of the bazaar: both are vast covered markets with branching wings where retailers display their wares in order to win the business of shoppers looking for bargains.

technology has radically altered some of the rules of business, the hustling culture of trading cities remains unchanged from previous epochs.

Many of the great merchant cities — Alexandria, medieval Cairo, Timbuktu in West Africa, Venice, New York and Hong Kong — were either ports of call or located on important trade routes. Their streets teeming with immigrants, merchant cities have tended to be open-minded and accepting of new cultures. After all, a city can't provide a big enough market for its own goods, so commerce is outward-directed. Unlike feudal or religious centers, merchant cities fostered the growth of an affluent middle class whose members participated in local government. In Venice, guilds and business associations provided social services and invested in the infrastructure required to maintain efficient commercial operations.

Because these cities have focused on trading goods and commodities that may be produced elsewhere, their business class grew to include financiers, insurers, bankers, accountants, lawyers, brokers and wholesalers — all entrepreneurial professions dedicated to lubricating commercial relationships. Lastly, merchant cities typically grow into enlightened centers of culture and learning, where the business classes become patrons of the arts and educational institutions. The great Italian Renaissance cities of Milan and Florence didn't have large populations like the megacities of the ancient world. Rather, their wealth and their subsequent cultural significance sprang from their "powerful commercial spirit," says Kotkin.[19]

Industrial Cities
In 1939, Bill Hewlett and Dave Packard, a pair of Stanford University graduate students, founded an electronics company

in a garage in Palo Alto, California. By the 1950s, their company, Hewlett-Packard, had become one of a growing club of high-tech manufacturers located in a sleepy exurban area south of San Francisco that came to be known as Silicon Valley.

Though Silicon Valley giants like HP or Apple bore little resemblance to previous generations of smoke-stack manufacturers, the area's concentration of high-tech firms transformed the Bay Area into an industrial metropolis, following a well-established pattern of urban development. Going back to the earliest days of the Industrial Revolution in England, certain city-regions came to be strongly identified with various manufacturing sectors. The American car industry took root in Detroit after Henry Ford established a carriage factory there in 1896. The steel and petrochemical industries clustered in cities like Pittsburgh, Hamburg and Hamilton — places where raw materials were easily accessible either by rail or water. American defense contractors, shipbuilders and aerospace firms congregated in the Los Angeles/San Diego corridor, where they could serve nearby naval and air force bases. And Chicago, a railway terminus strategically located between the farms of the midwest and the cities of the northeast, came to be known for its vast stockyards, slaughterhouses and meat-packing plants.

The template for the industrial city dates back to England in the 1850s, when Manchester and the Lancashire region turned into the epicenter of global manufacturing, with a proliferation of factories and cotton mills. Its population surged, the middle classes grew and the city's economy exploded as entrepreneurs gravitated toward these boom towns. Still, squalid living conditions for the working classes, coupled with extreme pollution, made death rates rise sharply and stoked political tensions.[20]

Industrial cities have proven to be vulnerable to environmental degradation and rapid shifts in global trade. Pittsburgh, by the 1940s, had become nearly uninhabitable due to air and water pollution, a situation that forced civic leaders to find ways of improving quality of life and diversifying the local economy. Cities like Detroit, Buffalo and parts of Los Angeles fell into decline as huge factories closed or relocated to urban areas with lower labor costs. In recent decades, those cities could be found in the so-called right-to-work states in the US south, the free trade *maquiladora* zones on the border between Mexico and Texas, and emerging Asian economies like Thailand, South Korea and India. Since the early 1990s, the booming cities in southeast China's five "special economic zones," as well as Beijing and Shanghai, have seen an unprecedented influx of foreign direct investment, leading to a huge buildup of manufacturing facilities and a sharp increase in the standard of living in these areas.

China, for all its economic dynamism, likely won't be immune to the restlessness of the global industrial sector, which will someday be searching elsewhere for low-wage city-regions that can provide workers for new factories.

Immigrant Cities
In the late 1980s, the government of Canada decided to triple its annual immigration target, from 85,000 people per year to roughly 250,000. The majority of newcomers have settled in three large cities: Vancouver, Montreal and Toronto.

As of the 2006 census, in fact, the Toronto region had become the most ethnically diverse metropolis in the world, with more than 45 percent of its residents born outside Canada. Even some of the world's most populous cities don't boast such diversity.[21]

Immigration is not new: the streets of some of history's great trading capitals were crowded with outsiders. Writing about Cairo in the sixteenth century, Anthony Tung says the city's "cosmopolitan streetscape held as many as 12,000 shops jammed with commercial activity from around the world. The city contained a Christian quarter, a Jewish quarter, a Greek quarter, an Egyptian quarter, a Turkish quarter and Bedouin quarters."[22]

Immigrants gravitate to cities in search of work and a better standard of living for their children. Migration is also a result of crises — people fleeing conflict, political repression and natural disaster. First-generation immigrants or refugees typically settle in ethnic enclaves, open businesses, build temples and establish community networks, usually with the goal of paving the way for their children to have the opportunity to put down firm roots in their new homes. Even relatively homogenous cities, like Tokyo, have enclaves of immigrants from Korea and China.

But in many cities, the immigrant story has been anything but straightforward. In some European countries, like France and Germany, migrant laborers, denied the full rights of citizenship, are a fixture of the urban underclass, clustered in low-income suburban ghettos with high unemployment rates. In Canada, immigrants contend with chronic shortages of affordable housing and barriers to entering the workforce. And in some large US cities, scarred by stark racial divisions, the presence of illegal immigrants, particularly Hispanics from Latin America, remains a politically and socially volatile issue. Lawmakers and city-dwellers grapple over questions such as whether the US-born children of illegal immigrants should be entitled to basic social services.

Global Cities

Since the 1960s, a new form of city-region has emerged on the world stage. The term "global cities," made popular by urban sociologist Saskia Sassen, refers to a series of megacities that have come to resemble one another in terms of their economic and political clout, advanced infrastructure and social diversity. Located on every continent, these cities function in a thoroughly globalized environment, operating at a level that extends beyond the traditional jurisdictional and geographical constraints placed on most metropolitan areas.

While the global city label came into common use in the early 1990s, megacities such as Imperial Rome, seventeenth-century Amsterdam and nineteenth-century London have exerted influence far beyond their urban boundaries. What's different today is the proliferation of such cities as a result of trade liberalization and mass urbanization.

Global cities share many key traits. They are, first and foremost, centers of investment and banking, which support large professional service sectors, including accounting and law firms, financial advisers and advertising agencies. The media, trans-national corporations and international organizations establish headquarters in global cities. These places are also home to leading research institutions, universities, national cultural venues and prominent arts festivals. Their residents and businesses are served by modern infrastructure — major international airports, rapid transit systems, well-maintained highways, state-of-the-art container ports, and extensive communications and information technology systems.

In some ways, global cities are microcosms of the evolution of the world's rapidly growing urban population. As with the powerful merchant cities of the past, global cities are destinations for immigrants. But despite their wealth, global cities generate large and growing income gaps between rich and poor. They attract mobile professionals who can demand "global" salaries that are on par with those in other leading cities. At the same time, global cities have post-industrial economies. They have shrinking middle classes, and many of the immigrants who flock to them end up working in low-wage service sectors — restaurants, hotels, offices, construction sites, cleaning agencies.

While most of the world's global cities are located in North America, Europe and the powerhouse economies of the Far East, their ranks have come to include booming cities in developing countries like India. Since the early 1990s, Mumbai (formerly Bombay) has become a magnet for foreign firms, including finance and professional service companies, and international hotel chains. Many of these firms set up in Mumbai's newly created district, Nariman Point. It is distinguished by its sleek office towers and broad streets, and contrasts with Mumbai's older commercial districts, which are dominated by colonial architecture and domestic businesses.[23]

Such development patterns illustrate how global cities are increasingly tethered to one another through links between the offices of international firms and the instantaneous movement of investment capital. Saskia Sassen points out that global cities function as "strategic command centers," presiding over the operations of decentralized manufacturing operations located on supply chains that span the earth.[24]

In light of this evolution in the shape of the world's richest cities, urban experts have posed difficult questions about the relationship between these places and the relatively impoverished rest of the world. Some predict that the world's thirty or so leading cities will someday eclipse the G-8 (the Group of Eight governments of Canada, France, Germany, Italy, Japan, Russia, the United Kingdom and the United States) and take command of the world's economic levers.[25] Sassen asks who may rightfully lay claim to a city once it has been pressed into service by an international elite. The abstraction of globalization, she notes, takes on a concrete form in global cities, where the extremes of wealth and poverty are not only highly visible, but have created the conditions for a new era of urban class conflict. Indeed, in recent years, some affluent cities have experienced clashes between police and radical antipoverty activists or migrant workers, as well as labor disputes pitting thousands of poorly paid hospitality industry employees against hotel chains that cater to business travelers and affluent tourists. Such confrontations are bound to play out on the stage of the twenty-first century city, characterized as it is by extreme social contrasts and contested spaces.[26]

Chapter 3
Sprawl Happens

In the prosperous decades after the end of World War II, the shape of many Western cities — especially those in North America — underwent a radical shift that sharply altered the way millions of people experience their urban environments. Quite abruptly, compact urban development patterns established over centuries gave way to something very new and decentralized. Cities became dispersed, low-slung, unfocused. Traditional commercial districts and avenues gave way to shopping malls surrounded by parking lots and anchored by department stores.

Postwar affluence allowed millions of young families to buy homes in newly developed suburbs.[1] But these communities didn't look or function like earlier generations of residential areas. In place of apartments, tenements and cramped row houses built for blue-collar workers on dense city blocks, the new subdivisions were spacious, with a backyard and a driveway for each home. Instead of the traditional grid, the streets curved and wound around, often ending in cul-de-sacs.

The common denominator in this new pattern of urban living was the privately owned automobile. Though cars had been commercially available long before World War II, they tended to be luxury items, especially through the Great

Depression and the austerity of the war years. But in the 1950s and 1960s, the car became a mass-market consumer good, providing families with the kind of personal mobility and independence they had never enjoyed before.

For centuries, cities had retained a physically compact form partly because there were limited transportation options available to inhabitants and merchants. People had very practical reasons to live within walking distance of shops and the local market. Then, with the advent of streetcars and subways in the late nineteenth century, new suburbs grew up in the vicinity of transit stops and along tram routes.

But the family car changed everything. Suddenly, the long-standing constraints on daily travel disappeared, and that fact of life altered the way city-dwellers moved through urban spaces. Where city-dwellers once favored proximity out of necessity, the new suburbanites required only ease of parking and readily available gas stations. For the breadwinner, it no longer mattered how far one lived from the office or the factory.

These changes brought about an entirely new way of thinking about urban form. First of all, the new suburbs took up a lot more space — the lots were larger, which meant they required much more infrastructure, such as water mains, sewer systems, asphalt for street surfacing. Second, municipal officials and road engineers ushered in what could be described as a revolution in the way cities planned their main streets. Before the advent of the car, the main street was as much a destination as a thoroughfare. Main streets were lined with shops, offices, government buildings, factories, apartments. They, in turn, were used by pedestrians, cyclists, cars, delivery vehicles, carriages and trams. As automobile travel rewired the city, the main street or arterial evolved into a much more functional piece of the urban environment, dedicated increasingly to the needs of cars.

One of the hallmarks of postwar development is the so-called separation of uses. Beginning in the late nineteenth century, social reformers like the English planner Ebenezer Howard began advocating a new type of city that allowed families with young children to escape from the disease-ridden, polluted industrial slums downtown. While some "garden city" suburbs were built in the early decades of the twentieth century, these ideas really came into their own during the postwar suburban boom, and were made possible only with the

Gated Communities

Beginning in the 1980s, a distinctive type of subdivision began appearing in and around the fringes of some North American cities. By outward appearance, most gated communities look like conventional luxury residential developments, well-appointed, with attractive landscaping and elegant homes, often built around a three-hole golf course and other recreational amenities. But these communities are private — visitors have to enter through a round-the-clock security checkpoint, and only with an invitation. Unlike conventional neighborhoods, the internal roads are privately owned and therefore inaccessible to the general public.

According to 2004 US census data, about 10 percent of primary homes worth more than $500,000* are situated in gated communities. But among luxury homes built between 2000 and 2003, the figure rises to 17 percent — evidence, according to Forbes Magazine, that a growing number of high-end buyers are choosing to live behind secured barriers.[2] Other estimates suggest that about 4 million Americans live in gated communities, which account for 11 percent of all new housing developments.[3]

Developers position most of these projects as "adult communities" that are marketed to seniors, retirees and homebuyers fleeing from crime and other urban ills. The additional safety comes with a price beyond monthly common-area main-

advent of mass car ownership. In newly planned modernist suburbs, like Toronto's Don Mills, municipal officials physically segregated residential areas from shopping malls and office or industrial "parks," marking a sharp departure from centuries of urban development patterns. The car allowed such separation of uses. But as suburbs grew and spread even further into the hinterland, car travel ceased to be a liberating convenience and became a necessity, even for the simplest of tasks — taking kids to school or fetching milk from the store.

The outward push of the postwar city has produced ever-worsening traffic congestion. Major arterials and highways in

tenance fees. In some gated communities, homeowners must adhere to a range of legally enforceable restrictions relating to noise, the external décor of their homes, even whether vehicles can be left in driveways overnight. What is more, the security cordon excludes canvassers and politicians campaigning for public office, raising concerns among civil libertarians.

Nor is this just an American trend. In recent years, gated communities have cropped up in Canada, the United Kingdom, Europe, Latin America, Africa and the Far East. In the megacities of the developing world, wealthy residents, senior government officials and foreign diplomats have long secluded themselves inside privately guarded enclaves or, as they're known in South Africa, "security villages." Urban commentator Mike Davis, in *Planet of Slums*, cites exclusive outlying suburbs in cities like São Paulo, Bangalore, Johannesburg and Lagos, which are linked by special highways to office districts. The residential areas are protected from the outside world by gates and security services, meaning that the inhabitants are able to isolate themselves from urban poverty — a process he describes as "a fundamental reorganization of metropolitan space, involving a drastic diminution of the intersections between the lives of the rich and the poor."[4]

*All dollars are US dollars.

large cities are chronically clogged because suburban residents have no real alternatives but to drive everywhere.

That's not the only vicious circle evident in the current pattern of suburban growth. On the "exurban" fringes of many large cities, developers have taken to building luxury homes — sometimes known as McMansions — on large lots located well beyond suburban boundaries. Some consumers are drawn to these homes because they've grown weary of older suburban areas, with all their congestion. Meanwhile, other homeowners organize themselves to fight any new development projects, especially those that

---

Density Debunked

In the early 1960s, writer Jane Jacobs, a trenchant urban philosopher and local activist, became one of the first commentators to counter prevailing opinion about the push by governments to build low-density suburbs. For decades, urban reformers had argued that dense cities led to slums, crime and other social problems linked to overcrowding. "[H]igh densities of dwellings and overcrowding of dwellings are often confused," replied Jacobs in her classic treatise, *The Death and Life of Great American Cities*. High densities, she observed, meant large numbers of dwelling units per acre, whereas overcrowding meant "too many people in a dwelling for the number of rooms it contains." She accused urban reformers of confusing the two measures as a means of justifying slum clearance campaigns in working-class districts of cities like Boston. She pointed out that simply because a neighborhood is dense, it isn't necessarily afflicted by disease, poverty or other symptoms of social decay. "The facts," as she said, "are more complicated."[5]

While Jacobs succeeded in debunking some of the prevailing myths about density, many homeowner associations continue to oppose intensification and high-density development, insisting that a concentrated influx of new residents places undue burdens on municipal and social infrastructure. Often, though, such arguments are mainly a pretext for middle-class opposition to high rises or affordable housing projects.

provide affordable or high-rise housing. The result is a leap-frog development pattern — a term that describes how subdivisions spring up further and further from built-up urban areas.

This process, known as "suburban sprawl," has become the defining feature of postwar cities in North America and, increasingly, in affluent suburban areas around large Western European cities, such as Frankfurt, which saw the population of its core drop as growth in its outlying regions surged between the 1970s and late 1990s.[6] According to one definition, cities are said to sprawl when their physical boundaries grow faster than the population. Another measure of sprawl involves density, meaning the number of dwelling units per unit of area (see box opposite). Sprawling cities, like Atlanta or Houston, have very low densities, while compact urban areas, such as Manhattan, Hong Kong or downtown Vancouver, have extremely high densities, as do many of the teeming megacities of the developing world. Unlike high-rise cities, the density in some huge developing world metropolises is a function of overcrowding and the unchecked proliferation of substandard housing (see table next page).

Besides the environmental harm caused by sprawl, many urban experts and critics cite a range of problems relating to this pattern of development:

• *Infrastructure.* The cost of building and maintaining municipal infrastructure is higher in low-density areas than in compact cities. More materials are required for roads and sewers; garbage trucks consume more fuel because the routes are longer, etc.

• *Inefficient Use of Land.* A hallmark of sprawl is an abundance of vacant or underused land such as scrubby strips around industrial buildings or at the edge of major roads.

• *Cost of Living.* Suburban living is expensive. Houses are larg-

Selected Densities of the World's 250 Largest Cities

	Density Rank	Population /km2
Mumbai	1	29,650
Lagos	4	18,150
Seoul	6	16,700
Bogotá	9	13,500
Shanghai	10	13,400
Delhi	13	11,050
Kinshasa	14	10,650
São Paulo	25	9,000
Singapore	29	8,350
Hong Kong	39	6,350
London	43	5,100
Los Angeles	90	2,750
Toronto	97	2,650
Frankfurt	105	2,300
Sydney	113	2,100
New York City*	114	2,050
Copenhagen	117	1,850
Miami	121	1,700
Calgary	139	1,250
Houston	149	1,150
Atlanta	203	700

Source: CityMayors.com ranking[7]
*Metropolitan New York

er and cost more to heat or cool. Most travel involves a car, so families need to finance two or more vehicles, including gas, insurance and maintenance costs. In some sprawling cities, like Houston, average car-related costs exceed all other household expenditures, including housing.

• *Productivity.* Chronic suburban road congestion exacts a toll on businesses and individuals. Factories lose money when trucks bringing materials are delayed in traffic. Individuals may sacrifice several hours per day commuting, leading to missed appointments, road rage incidents, a loss of family time, even health problems (see Sprawl and Obesity).

But not everyone agrees with these indictments. In his 1991 treatise on suburban economic growth, *Edge City,* Joel Garreau pointed out that these outlying areas had ceased to be bedroom communities. He coined the phrase "edge city" to describe fast-emerging commercial clusters springing up on the fringes of large metropolitan regions. These areas, with their industrial/office parks and research campuses, were attracting a new generation of entrepreneurs, especially in emerging high-tech sectors. In Garreau's view, these edge cities represented an exciting new urban frontier, not a wasteland.[8]

Looking back, Robert Bruegmann, a professor of art history and architecture at the University of Illinois at Chicago, argues that cities have long spread into the agricultural hinterland, filling in the rural gaps between adjacent towns and villages, a pattern that marked the evolution of London, England. In *Sprawl: A Compact History,* Bruegmann challenges many of the familiar arguments about sprawl. He observes that the urban population is constantly churning, as newcomers move into the city to find work while city-dwellers relocate outward when they can afford it. After World War II, manufacturers increasingly moved out of the core and into the suburbs, which helped accelerate the suburban exodus.

In recent decades, core areas were gentrified, as homeowners fixed up historic neighborhoods and developers erected lux-

Sprawl and Obesity

The contemporary suburb traces its roots to the visions of nineteenth-century reformers who wanted to create healthier urban environments as a respite for laborers trapped in heavily polluted industrial cities. But there's mounting evidence that the car-dependent suburban lifestyle may be contributing to the epidemic of obesity in Western countries like the US and Canada.

In 2004, researchers with the University of British Columbia and the Centers for Disease Control and Prevention pointed to a "strong link" between time spent driving and obesity. They calculated that "[e]very additional 30 minutes spent in a car each day translates into a 3 percent greater chance of being obese."[9]

On its own, that conclusion makes intuitive sense. But the study also showed a connection between car use and urban form. Surveying the travel habits of almost 11,000 people living in the Atlanta region, the researchers found greater car dependence in "disconnected" parts of the city, that is, areas where uses are strictly separated, meaning that people must drive between homes, schools, offices, services and malls. By contrast, in more "connected" communities, where these various uses were not segregated from one another, the residents not only drove less, but seemed to be less likely to suffer from obesity-related diseases.

The study's conclusions: mixed-use communities are inherently healthier because they provide residents with more opportunities to get out of their cars.

ury high rises in downtowns. That process, Bruegmann writes, "is closely connected to sprawl at the edge. As the number of working-class families moving to the edge for cheaper land prices have mounted, affluent families have been increasingly less willing to move farther outward, particularly since many prestigious jobs in business, law, medicine and the cultural and non-profit worlds either remained or have been newly created in the traditional city centers."[10]

What's more, sprawl is apparent in major metropolitan

areas in Europe, such as Île-de-France (the region surrounding the City of Paris) as well as cities in Spain and Italy. Northern European city-regions, by contrast, have made political decisions to control growth with environmentally sustainable planning, which enjoys far less public support in North America, where cash is king. In Munich and Hamburg, for example, the exurban clusters on the periphery of both cities tend to be dense and separated from one another by greenbelts.

New Urbanism, Intensification and Smart Growth

As postwar development accelerated, the political backlash against car-oriented sprawl began to gain traction. Environmentalists, reform-minded planners, architects, city-dwellers and even some developers began to debate new approaches to containing the seemingly unstoppable expansion of North American cities. They would point to some European and Asian cities, which remained denser than their North American counterparts. There were a range of reasons, including tighter regulations on development, more spending on transit and the public's continued willingness to live in the mid-rise apartments that dominate the core areas of most European cities and high-density metropolises like Singapore.

The contrast underscored the reality that in most North American cities, powerful developers and landowners wield undue influence in the sphere of local politics, whereas urban planning in other developed nations (e.g., the Scandinavian countries) is tethered much more closely to regional and national policy agendas, such as environmental protection, energy efficiency and cultural preservation. In Stockholm, for example, the municipality had been acquiring land on the outskirts of the city for much of the twentieth century, always with an eye to creating relatively dense, highly planned communities linked by subway or commuter rail to the urban core.

The 1990s brought renewed interest in transit-oriented planning in North America after decades of laissez-faire, car-focused development. The New Urbanists, a reform movement of architects and planners, criticized the conventional subdivision, with its rows of identical homes with protruding garages, over-wide streets and dearth of local shops. Working with forward-looking builders, the New Urbanists laid out a vision for a more pedestrian-friendly form of neighborhood planning, one characterized by features such as conventional blocks instead of cul-de-sacs, rear laneways instead of huge front yard garages, and forward-facing homes with porches. Many builders (including the Disney corporation's real estate arm) quickly caught on to the attractive cosmetic features of the New Urbanists' neo-traditional designs, but these subdivisions remained car-dependent, isolated from stores, schools, offices and transit.

Other cities decided to counter sprawl by making drastic changes in their planning rules to encourage "intensification." In Vancouver and Toronto, visionary planners eased land-use restrictions and other regulations governing downtown land, much of which had been zoned for commerce and industry. The relaxing of the land use rules allowed developers to convert warehouses into upscale lofts and develop slim high-rise towers in areas that had been set aside for office buildings. As a result, both cities saw a surge in high-density downtown residential development, as upscale condo builders hustled to buy old factories and fallow lots. While such reforms have created populous new vertical communities that are close to transit, shops and offices, they have also triggered a backlash among the residents of older downtown working-class districts, who fear that gentrification and redevelopment will render their neighborhoods unaffordable.

More recently, the "smart growth" movement has emerged as a more comprehensive approach to containing sprawl. Often initiated by state or provincial governments, smart growth strategies concentrate new development in existing urban areas rather than allow cities to continue expanding into the countryside. Though relatively new to North America, such principles have been in use by European urban planners for decades.

Smart growth measures include tax incentives for redeveloping derelict areas and so-called brownfield sites (former industrial properties that have been abandoned and may be contaminated), investments in rapid transit, and urban growth boundaries. Early political advocates, such as former Maryland governor Parris Glendening, also used the state budget to advance smart growth plans. Glendening reduced highway spending and targeted infrastructure grants — for schools, housing, water and sewer services — to urban districts that had been designated as growth areas.

Indeed, the most crucial aspect of smart growth is effective regional planning. Experts point to Portland, Oregon, as the gold standard among North American cities. In the late 1970s, local and state politicians decided to fight sprawl by establishing a regional government and a firm urban growth boundary. Metro Portland included the City of Portland and a constellation of twenty-five neighboring municipalities. As a regional government, it had the power to concentrate development, deliver regional services and build the kind of light-rail transit network that doesn't exist in most US cities of its size.

In recent years, however, Portland has grown out to its urban growth boundary, and has had to approve an expansion. In fact, some critics point out that its overall population density isn't any better than some larger North American cities, such as Los Angeles and Toronto, while property rights activists have challenged the legality of Oregon's tough anti-sprawl laws.

But smart growth isn't just about rebalancing the way cities develop. It's also about restoring the notion that our urban spaces should have a "sense of place." Critics of postwar planning, like journalist James Howard Kunstler, condemn much of what has been built in North American suburbs in the postwar period. Huge shopping malls, clogged arterial roads lined with burger joints and muffler shops, and vast subdivisions filled with nearly identical homes — these are symptoms of a low-density suburban environment planned almost exclusively around the needs of the car. The result, all too often, is a junk-ridden landscape that lacks vitality or any sense of distinctiveness. "Suburbia fails us in large part because it is so abstract," Kunstler writes. "It is the idea of a place rather than a place."[11]

Chapter 4
Environment and Energy

In an uncertain era of climate change, city-dwellers will come under ever-growing pressure to reduce the impact their lifestyles are having on the global environment. North Americans and many Europeans have become accustomed to hopping in the car to get a carton of milk. They don't think twice about buying produce grown halfway around the world and shipped to abundantly stocked supermarkets. Climate change will require the residents of big cities to rethink these commonplace habits.

As we saw in Chapter 3, most North American cities are low-density metropolitan regions characterized by an older, compact core surrounded by a sprawling landscape of subdivisions, malls and industrial parks. Such development patterns are producing a vicious cycle of energy dependence and environmental degradation.

Spacious suburban homes on large lots consume enormous amounts of energy. Their owners depend on cars and light trucks to travel around the city because transit isn't convenient. Vehicle emissions fill the atmosphere with microparticles and greenhouse gases (GHGs). In comparison to smaller downtown homes or apartments, large dwellings require lots of oil, gas and electricity, the production of which may involve burning high-emission fuels, like coal.

Large lawns, in turn, require generous amounts of fertilizer that leach into the water table. Water supplies are depleted because we build homes with too many bathrooms, run our dishwashers when they're half full and overwater our gardens. The abundance of residential storage space encourages the over consumption of consumer goods, and these, in turn, produce mountains of packaging waste, much of which ends up buried in municipal landfills.

Greenfield development, meanwhile, destroys habitats, woodlands, wetlands and agricultural land. The disappearance of farms near cities means that food must be shipped over longer distances — a process that entails more GHG emissions. Large expanses of pavement — the ingredients for which come from gravel quarries and cement factories — damage watersheds because rainwater runoff, rather than being absorbed and filtered by the environment, is shunted into storm sewers, leaving local ecosystems parched. The loss of trees, coupled with overuse of heat-absorbing materials, such as shingles, raises the ambient temperature, forcing urban dwellers to turn up their air conditioners and consume more power.

There's no doubt we have been building increasingly unsustainable cities. Yet urban regions have always faced formidable, and frequently deadly, environmental challenges. Throughout history, civic authorities grappled with tenacious problems that affected city-dwellers' quality of life: securing sources of fresh food and water, building cities that are resistant to natural disasters, safely disposing of human waste, and managing the garbage generated by daily life in urban neighborhoods.

Poor air quality was a major issue, especially in industrial cities. In England, for example, the use of cheap bitumen coal for household furnaces and stoves dates back hundreds of

The Urban Heat Island Effect

Big cities tend to be warmer than surrounding rural areas. According to the US Environmental Protection Agency, "heat islands form as vegetation is replaced by asphalt and concrete for roads, buildings and other structures necessary to accommodate growing populations. These surfaces absorb — rather than reflect — the sun's heat, causing surface temperatures and overall ambient temperatures to rise."[1]

In large metropolitan areas, the urban heat island (UHI) can account for a 1 to 6-degree Celsius increase in the local temperature. Moreover, these spikes vary sharply within individual cities, depending on the amount of local green space. That's why a mall parking lot will always feel far warmer than a residential street with older shade trees.

While UHIs lead to increased air conditioner use, and therefore greater power consumption, this phenomenon has an even more serious impact on urban health. Heat is an important ingredient in the production of smog-related ozone, a gas that can damage lung tissue and reduce lung capacity. Children, seniors and the poor tend to be more vulnerable to severe heat-related illnesses. During a heat wave in 1995, more than 700 people in Chicago — many of them elderly — died due to heat exposure and dehydration.

With growing concern about energy consumption and climate change, many cities are looking for ways to counter the UHI with various strategies, including the installation of "green roofs," the use of heat-reflecting roofing materials and tree-planting campaigns. Such measures, however, are far more effective when combined with development policies that encourage compact urban form and large-scale investments in public transit.

years. By the eighteenth century, London's air was notoriously acrid, as the particulate-heavy smoke mixed with fog to create a toxic haze that would linger over the city. Monarchs and parliamentary politicians repeatedly attempted to ban the use of the cheap coal, but with little success. The Industrial Revolution in the nineteenth century made the problem worse — not just in London, but in cities with newly built factories. Only after a particularly lethal bout of London fog, which was responsible for 4,000 deaths in 1952, did the British government enact tough air pollution laws.[2]

In recent decades, governments in North America, Europe, Australia and Japan have tried to improve urban air quality by imposing more stringent emission controls on cars, trucks, smokestack factories and municipal solid waste incinerators. Yet sprawling urban areas, such as Los Angeles, continue to endure frequent smog days.

Water quality is another age-old challenge for city regions. Dense urban neighborhoods, because of cramped and unhygienic living conditions, were vulnerable to fast-moving epidemics, such as smallpox, cholera and bubonic plague.[3] Some of these diseases spread through municipal water/sewer systems contaminated with bacteria found in human and animal waste.

The earliest sanitary sewers were built over 5,000 years ago. Roman engineers made remarkable strides in water infrastructure, but much of their knowledge disappeared during the Dark Ages (see A Brief History of Sewers, page 130). It was only in the nineteenth century that municipalities and public health authorities began separating storm water and sewer drains and replacing outdoor latrines. They built sophisticated water filtration and sewage treatment plants, introduced chlorination and established vaccination programs. The results were evident almost immediately. For example, in Toronto after a determined campaign to modernize the city's sewage and water systems in the 1920s, infant mortality rates plunged, from 140 per thousand to 63 per thousand within a decade.[4]

But if cities in the developed world have largely solved the hygiene issues associated with urban water supply, another potentially devastating issue has come to the fore: shortages due either to drought, overuse or unsustainable population growth. In parts of Australia, the southwest US, and sprawling urban regions like Atlanta, water shortages have become increasingly acute in recent years, forcing municipal and regional agencies to scramble for additional supplies and even consider the prospect of water rationing. Las Vegas, one of the fast-growing metropolitan regions in the US, relies on water from the Colorado River, which has experienced falling levels for several years. "We've decoupled land use from water use," a Colorado water official told the *New York Times*. "Water is the limiting resource in the West."[5]

Environmental Degradation in the South's Megacities

If urban sprawl and consumerism have produced environmental problems linked to wealth and overconsumption, the megacities of Asia, Africa and Latin America are facing devastating ecological and health crises from overcrowding, slope erosion, resource depletion and inadequate sanitation.

Lagos, Nigeria, is the world's sixth-largest city, with 15 million inhabitants. Some of the city's slums, writes journalist George Packer, are built in an intensely polluted lagoon, where "fishermen and market women paddle dugout canoes on water as black and viscous as an oil slick... Smoldering hills of sawdust landfill send white smoke across the bridge, which mixes with diesel exhaust from the traffic." Garbage is everywhere — lining the streets, or piled into looming mounds that "steam with the combustion of natural gases."[6] There's virtually no piped water, meaning that wealthy residents bore their own wells while the poor, who continue to stream into the city at a rate of 600,000 per year, pay for buckets of filthy water.

Throughout the developing world, the impoverished inhabitants of megacities contend with a staggering range of environmental disasters. Shanty towns are built on unstable slopes vulnerable to landslides and earthquakes. In low-lying cities in countries like Bangladesh, slums spread into flood plains. Because land in such cities is scarce, squatters build shacks near factories or the shores of contaminated lakes.

The provision of water and sanitation has emerged as a daunting challenge. In cities like Kinshasa, Nairobi, Manila and Jakarta, millions of poor residents have limited access to sewer systems, toilets and running water. While even the poorest countries say they are upgrading urban water systems, "millions of [city-dwellers] suffer from waterborne diseases, indicating that they do not have adequate access to safe drinking water as officially reported," says the UN Habitat's 2006-2007 report on the state of the world's cities.[7] In addition, an estimated 600 million urban-dwellers globally lack even basic forms of sanitation.[8]

Traffic, in turn, has created permanent gridlock in many megacities in the developing world, leading to a drastic deterioration in air quality and a spike in deaths associated with heart and lung disease. Air pollution in developing world cities is estimated to be a factor in more than 2 million premature deaths each year, half due to indoor cooking fires. Industrialization is the other major cause. A World Bank study concludes that China has sixteen of the twenty worst-ranked cities for air quality, in large part because the country is building hundreds of new coal-fired electrical generators to keep pace with demand driven by surging economic growth. The result: China is now the world's second-largest emitter of greenhouse gases after the US and will soon be in top spot.[9]

The proliferation of megacity garbage presents the third devastating environmental dilemma. As Packer observes, "the most widely available commodity in Lagos is garbage. It is an engine of growth in the underworld of the city's informal economy, a vast sector with an astonishing volume of supply."[10]

Unlike modern municipal waste management facilities (meticulously engineered landfill sites, solid waste incinerators, or facilities that generate compost from organics), the trash produced in many cities in the developing world ends up in reeking, unstable heaps. Yet in places like Lagos, Manila and Buenos Aires, massive municipal dumps have created a labor-intensive recycling economy. The districts around these landfills are dominated by scrap companies that sell certain materials — copper wire, plastics, printer cartridges — to reprocessing firms. The scrap companies buy their raw materials from garbage pickers who spend their days scrambling over the piles with sacks, looking for the right type of trash, which they'll sell for a few dollars each day.

The working conditions are treacherous, as pickers, many of them children, are constantly exposed to toxic runoff, acrid smoke, or accidents involving bulldozers and trucks. In July 2000, Manila's 20-hectare (50-acre) Payatas dump, then the height of a 13-storey building, abruptly capsized, killing hundreds of scavengers who lived in the shanty towns at its base. Manila's population has ballooned from 1.5 million to 15 million since 1950. "The trash, accumulated over three decades, had been piled up to a 70-degree angle, and the rain-saturated mountain…collapsed," writes journalist Matthew Power in his account of the dump and the impoverished garbage pickers who see it as their livelihood. Payatas continues to operate.[11]

Greening the City

While compounding environmental catastrophes have made living conditions in such megacities increasingly nightmarish, the mathematical reality is that wealthy nations consume a *disproportionate* share of the world's energy and natural resources. For example, rich nations consume about ten times as much water per capita as poor nations.[12] Yet even among affluent nations, resource consumption varies significantly. Canada ranks at the top of the list for per capita energy use, not far ahead of the US, whose rates are almost twice as high as Europe and Japan.

While much environmental damage — such as overfishing, deforestation and habitat destruction due to excessive clear-cutting — occurs outside urban areas, there's nonetheless a strong connection between cities in the developed world and climate change. The reason is that wealthy nations are heavily urbanized, so the way these cities grow has a direct bearing on the pace of global warming, which in turn is already causing havoc in populous low-lying cities.

Urban form plays a critical role in determining a city's overall energy consumption. Car-oriented sprawl gobbles up energy and thus fuels climate change. By contrast, dense urban regions like Tokyo are far more energy efficient. Dwelling units are smaller and require less energy. Transit is more cost-effective. As well, there are opportunities to ride or walk that don't exist in suburban areas. As David Owen commented in the *New Yorker* in 2004, "Dense urban centers offer one of the few plausible remedies for some of the world's most discouraging environmental ills.... To borrow a term from the jargon of computer systems, dense cities are scalable, while sprawling

Total World Energy Consumption, 2004

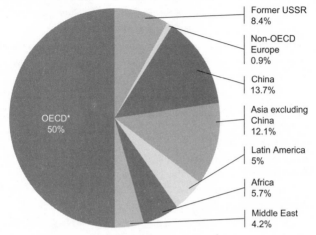

- Former USSR 8.4%
- Non-OECD Europe 0.9%
- China 13.7%
- Asia excluding China 12.1%
- Latin America 5%
- Africa 5.7%
- Middle East 4.2%
- OECD* 50%

*Twenty-five of the thirty members of the Organisation for Economic Co-operation and Development (OECD) are considered high-income countries by the World Bank.
Source: International Energy Agency, "Key World Energy Statistics, 2006." www.iea.org/textbase/nppdf/free/2006/key2006.pdf.

suburbs are not. The environmental challenge we face, at the current stage of our assault on the world's non-renewable resources, is not how to make our teeming cities more like the pristine countryside. The true challenge is how to make other settled places more like Manhattan."[13]

That transformation will depend heavily on whether we change the way we think about transit, transportation and land-use planning, which is the subject of Chapter 5. But cities around the world are now pushing ahead with many forward-looking ideas that are beginning to reduce their overall impact on their environment.

Cities, Climate Change and Flooding

One of the most worrisome symptoms of climate change involves changes in the level of the earth's seas. Due to rising temperatures, polar ice caps and mountain glaciers have begun melting at an alarming rate, causing sea levels to rise. Around the world, hundreds of millions of people live in teeming urban regions that are built at or even below sea level, meaning that rising waters pose a dire threat to a significant proportion of the world's population. A 2007 report by the UK government predicted that by the end of the twenty-first century, storm "surges," rising sea levels and floods could displace 200 million people in twenty-two major city-regions around the world, from Manhattan to Mumbai.[14]

Climate change and rising ocean temperatures are also implicated in the proliferation of violent hurricanes. In August 2005, Hurricane Katrina pounded New Orleans, causing a catastrophic breach of the city's levees that left more than 1,300 people dead and thousands without homes.[15] (Some of the city was built on drained swamps in the flood plain of the Mississippi River.) New Orleans' poorest neighborhoods, many of them predominantly African-American, were most afflicted. In the wake of the disaster, it became clear that federal emergency management officials had failed to address problems with the levees, despite pleas from experts and municipal leaders.

Since Katrina, many affluent cities have begun planning to prevent such disasters, and their enormous potential for property damage. Singapore, for example, is looking at constructing dikes to protect itself in the coming decades. Its civil engineers asked the Netherlands for help.[16] In Holland, one of Europe's most urbanized nations, the low-lying northern provinces sit below sea level, having been reclaimed from the North Sea with an elaborate system of dikes, drainage canals and windmills. Dutch government officials are spending billions of dollars to upgrade the dike system so it can withstand the symptoms of climate change. But some innovative Dutch architects, those at the forefront of the eco-architecture movement, are developing lightweight homes that can be built without foundations on a hollow base. They can float in the event of a flood.[17]

Recycling Programs

During the past twenty years, many municipalities have introduced increasingly comprehensive recycling programs as a means of prolonging the lives of landfill sites. The volumes of garbage generated in big cities create the economies of scale needed to make recycling programs cost-effective (i.e., the expense of collecting, sorting and processing the material is less than the price recycling companies will pay to buy it).

In most cities, the collection is still done in very conventional ways: with trucks. But Swedish engineers devised an innovative automated approach to collecting such materials in the 1960s, and the technology has become increasingly attractive in recent years. "Centralsug" systems rely on networks of underground pneumatic tubes that can suck recyclable materials to sorting plants, thereby reducing truck emissions and the health hazards associated with waste handling. Residents feed newspapers, bottles and other recyclables into "inlets," located in apartment buildings or outdoors. According to Envac, the Swedish firm that pioneered the technology, about one in eight Stockholm households now rely on Centralsug collection systems, and the company is expanding aggressively in cities such as Barcelona, Vilnius, Hong Kong and Shanghai.

Thanks to advances in other recycling technologies, it is possible to find markets for an increasingly broad range of items once considered garbage. These include almost all paper products, beverage cartons, certain plastics, glass bottles and jars, cans, scrap metal, wire, waste oils and organics — a broad category of waste that includes kitchen scraps, used tissues, soiled disposable diapers and pet litter. Some cities also operate re-use facilities for large items such as furniture and appliances.

While programs for recycling newsprint, cardboard, scrap

metal and aluminum have been around for years, the range of secondary uses is growing rapidly, meaning that recycling programs are expanding steadily. For example, plastic in used pop bottles can now be used for synthetic fabrics such as fleece clothing, carpets and stuffing.[18] Old tires can be ground into crumbs for use in rubberized asphalt, pipes and mats.[19]

Meanwhile, concrete rubble from construction debris — which usually takes up a substantial volume of most municipal landfills — is being ground up for use as recycled aggregate in other construction projects, such as highway foundations and sidewalks.[20] Such measures reduce the demand for aggregate mines near urban areas to provide the raw material for paving and building supplies.

With organics, collected from homeowners in cities like Toronto and Halifax, the waste is sorted for contaminants (such as plastic bags and metals), cured and then used as an ingredient in the production of commercial compost.

Product Packaging Stewardship

Excessive packaging and used consumer goods are two large categories of waste that represent tough challenges for municipal waste management operations. With so many ordinary consumer products being shipped over long distances, packaging has become more complex and durable as manufacturers seek to protect their goods from damage. The result is overpackaging of items, many of which are double and triple wrapped (see The War on the Plastic Bag).

Europe has led the way in pushing for better product stewardship, meaning that producers should take more responsibility for all forms of waste generated by their goods. In 1994, the European Union enacted a packaging policy that set ambitious

The War on the Plastic Bag

The spring of 2007 may be remembered as the beginning of the end of the lowly plastic shopping bag. During a few charged months, legislators, consumers and retailers in California, Hong Kong and Ontario joined the growing roster of nations that have either banned plastic bags or imposed hefty fees (others include Australia, Ireland, Denmark, Bangladesh and South Africa[21]). The goal: persuade consumers to use re-usable sacks.

According to reusablebags.com, the annual global production of plastic bags is in the 500 billion to 1 trillion range. The bags take about 400 years to degrade. They clog landfills, block drains, get caught in tree branches and kill mammals and marine species that accidentally swallow them. They've been found virtually everywhere on the globe and are one of the most common sorts of garbage that wash up on beaches in coastal areas.

In 2002, Ireland introduced the equivalent of a twenty-five-cent levy on every plastic bag. It succeeded in reducing consumption by 95 percent. Other jurisdictions have followed suit. Some retailers have introduced reduction targets by promoting the use of cloth sacks and plastic bins. Voluntary retailer programs, however, haven't produced the large-scale reductions triggered by bag levies.

goals for reducing the amount of packaging used in the manufacturing process and maximizing the amount of waste packaging collected from homes, industries and commercial establishments. The EU's goal is for its member countries to be able to recover 60 percent of all packaging waste by 2008.[22]

Similarly, in the past decade, the EU has enacted a series of directives requiring manufacturers to set up systems to collect things like "end-of-life vehicles" as well as spent electrical appliances and electronic equipment, a.k.a. e-junk, such as used cell phones, printers and computers. Manufacturers are then required to absorb the cost of taking all that material, separating out the recyclable materials and disposing of the rest.

As with the packaging rules, the EU regulations set tough recovery rate targets, ranging from 70 percent to 80 percent of the total weight of the discarded goods.[23]

While many jurisdictions in North America are moving to collect e-junk and some are following EU moves on packaging restrictions, few have been as aggressive about forcing manufacturers — and, by implication, their shareholders and customers — to assume full financial responsibility for recycling the products they make.

Waste Disposal

In the 1980s, New York City became a symbol of everything that was wrong with garbage disposal, as barges piled high with the city's reeking trash floated aimlessly in the harbor, unable to find a place to dump their loads.

For smaller urban centers or those located in countries with an abundance of open space, burying garbage was the easiest way to deal with one of the most basic chores of local government. Advances in recycling programs and tougher waste management regulations mean a narrower range of materials is now trucked to landfills, while 40 percent to 60 percent of collected waste is "diverted." Many municipalities require landfills to be systematically "capped" and lined to reduce odors and contain the toxic liquid that leaches out of garbage. They use mechanical sorting systems to remove batteries and other hazardous wastes. Some cities, working with private energy companies, have developed systems to capture the methane that escapes from landfill sites and convert it to energy.

In spite of these changes, large North American cities like New York ship their trash over long distances because they've exhausted landfills that are closer to home.

Cities in smaller European and Asian countries can't rely as heavily on landfills because space is at such a premium. In those nations, many big cities rely on incinerators to burn garbage. Incineration was commonly used in North America, but it fell out of use by the 1980s following complaints that such facilities spewed carcinogenic ash, containing dioxins and heavy metals like mercury, on neighboring communities.

In the 1990s, the European Union passed stringent emission standards for solid waste incinerators. Several EU states, such as Denmark, Germany, France and Sweden, rely extensively on high-tech incinerators to dispose of the "residuals," meaning any garbage that can't be recycled. Some so-called waste-to-energy incinerators are also fitted out with steam-powered turbines that produce electricity.

While earlier incinerators were implicated in elevated cancer rates in downwind communities, modern scrubbers filter out virtually all toxins and trace metals. Some toxicologists say there's greater risk of ingesting dioxins from whole milk than from emissions produced by incinerators that comply with EU air quality standards. Yet for many environmentalists and some municipal politicians, incineration remains a controversial method of waste management. Opponents point to potential health risks, steep capital and operating costs, and the fact that incineration emissions continue to contribute to global warming. Moreover, when residents know their waste will be burned, they may have less incentive to recycle.

Urban Greening
In Chicago, environmentally minded municipal leaders have embarked on campaigns to plant millions of new trees in urban neighborhoods. Such measures are not merely aesthetic.

Trees provide shade and reduce ambient temperatures, which reduces the need for air conditioners (on hot days, air conditioners drive up energy demand, and the extra load on the electrical system contributes to worsening air quality). At the same time, deciduous trees and leafy plants absorb carbon dioxide and give off oxygen, so they play a vital role in limiting the release of greenhouse gases into the atmosphere.

Grassroots environmental organizations have long played an assertive role in finding ways to "green" cities; with escalating public concern over climate change, their ideas have finally entered the political mainstream.

Since the 1980s, for example, Toronto naturalists have systematically renaturalized the Don River watershed, an extensive ravine system that meanders through the city. This long-term project has involved extensive tree planting, slope stabilization and the establishment of wetlands and bird habitats, all in ravines in the middle of the city.

The guerilla gardening movement, in turn, has transformed abandoned properties or marginal swaths of municipal land into green spaces. Thousands of homeowners, meanwhile, think more environmentally about their own gardens. They plant native species and replace conventional lawns with leafy or flowering ground cover. The use of native species — plants that are indigenous to a particular climate — allows gardeners to limit their use of chemical fertilizers and pesticides, both of which are energy-intensive to manufacture and contribute to ground-water contamination. Indeed, some bold municipalities have gone the next step, passing bylaws that restrict the use of chemical fertilizers and encourage residents to limit excessive water use.

Urban Agriculture

Farmers' markets have become increasingly popular among upscale urbanites who prefer locally grown, organic produce to the imported fruit and vegetables available at supermarkets.

Such consumer tastes dovetail with older urban food trends: in cities like Toronto and Montreal in the postwar period, many immigrants from countries like Italy and Portugal grew their own fruit and vegetables in compact backyards or plot gardens provided by the municipality. In 2007, a Manhattan-based environmental education organization propelled urban farming to the next level by launching a solar-, wind- and biofuel-powered barge equipped with hydroponic greenhouses that will produce peppers and tomatoes while floating in the Hudson River.[24]

There's a strong environmental case to be made for urban agriculture: shipping produce through supply chains that extend thousands of kilometers consumes large quantities of energy in comparison to goods grown within a few hours' drive of the city. But in many cities in the developing world, urban agriculture plays a crucial role in providing poor inhabitants with a measure of security and additional income. Surveys done in twenty-four cities in Africa, Asia and Eastern Europe show that a significant proportion of households were involved in growing their own food. And according to UN Habitat, "in many cities, urban agriculture is a main or supplementary source of income or employment among low-income households."[25]

Yet there are risks associated with some forms of urban agriculture. Farms have been located on vacant industrial sites with high levels of chemical pollutants. And in Nairobi, news reports say that some urban farmers use untreated sewage to fertilize their produce, a practice that introduces contaminants into the food chain.[26]

Green Roofs

In all cities, flat roofs represent a vast supply of untapped urban space. Environmentalists increasingly regard these roofs as a new frontier that can be harnessed to cut energy consumption, carbon dioxide emissions and radiant heat created by traditional roofing materials, such as asphalt shingles.

A growing number of ecologically minded property owners are putting "green roofs" on the roofs of their buildings. These projects involve the installation of a sustainable elevated ecosystem that will help insulate buildings and absorb carbon dioxide. Green roofs are made of layers of soil or growing medium and are often planted with wind-resistant native species. They require irrigation systems and impermeable substructures that prevent water from leaking into the building beneath. Studies by Environment Canada have found that the insulating properties of a green roof can reduce both heat loss in the winter and air conditioning use in the summer.

Environmentally conscious European countries like Germany have led the way with green roof construction, but some North American cities, such as Chicago and Washington DC, are seeing rapid growth, thanks to the introduction of municipal policies and grants that encourage such ventures. As of 2007, the city of Chicago had 93,000 square meters (1,001,044 square feet) of installed green roofs and another 180,000 square meters (1,937,504 square feet) under construction – a total equivalent to the area of more than 30 football fields.[27]

Alternative Energy

Urban rooftops represent a largely untapped supply of renewable energy, in the form of wind and solar power. Since the 1970s, dedicated environmentalists have been rigging up solar-powered water heaters or photovoltaic panels on the roofs of their homes or apartments, but the cost of the equipment has prevented solar power from breaking into the consumer mainstream. With both wind and solar energy, technological advances and rapidly growing markets in Europe, California and Japan are driving down equipment costs.

Wind firms in Portland and Chicago are developing small-scale quiet turbines that can be installed on the tops of office towers, institutional buildings and even homes built in windy areas, where these fixtures won't have to compete with trees and overhead wires.[28] But some scientists remain skeptical, arguing that small turbines (which measure a few meters in height, compared to the large-scale turbines on wind farms that can be twenty or thirty storeys high) won't generate enough power to offset the cost of making them.

The urban solar power market is much further ahead. Since the mid-1990s, the demand for photovoltaic equipment has been expanding by 35 percent per year; by 2006, the global solar market was worth $10 billion, with much of the activity coming from Japan and Germany. Competition among solar equipment manufacturers has become increasingly intense as large players enter the field and invest significant sums in new research and production facilities.[29]

Germany and Japan, the market leaders, both adopted proactive alternative energy policies in the late 1990s. California has announced that it will spend close to $4 billion by 2017 to promote solar energy through tax incentives and rebates. In fact, a growing number of North American residential developers have begun selling new homes equipped with solar thermal panels and photovoltaic (PV) cells, especially in the sunny southwestern states. As the *Christian Science Monitor* reported in 2004: "[S]olar power is gaining a toehold in the most unlikely of places — the world of SUVs, big-screen TVs, and two-fridge families — the 'burbs.' And if it can gain acceptance there, some analysts say, the technology is on the cusp of widespread acceptance. 'Even suburbia is starting to go solar,' says Richard Perez, publisher of *Home Power* magazine, the bible of the home-renewable energy crowd. 'Some new houses and subdivisions are being planned this way. It's not really common yet, but it's happening.'"[30]

Yet the future of solar power will go well beyond residential installations. Large-scale solar farms and concentrators have been operating in California for years, and such facilities are being built in Ontario and Spain. The European Union is working with Algeria on a plan to construct massive solar farms in the Sahara, which could theoretically meet most of the electricity needs of Europe, the Middle East and North Africa.[31] In the US, meanwhile, some solar energy firms are targeting commercial and industrial landlords, offering to install panels on the roofs of big-box stores, distribution centers and factories. It's a huge market, given the proliferation of low-slung buildings on the peripheries of so many cities. One company, Baltimore's SunEdison, has signed up hundreds of corporate customers with an innovative approach: SunEdison owns, operates and maintains the solar equipment while the property owner signs a twenty-year contract to purchase the power generated on the roof at a fixed rate. That way, the customers don't have to worry about the capital costs and they save on their energy bills as the price of conventional electricity rises over time.

Sustainable Architecture

When we think about the sources of urban environmental stress, we envision gridlocked highways and factories spewing smoke. But cities, by their nature, are filled with buildings that have been constructed in ways that inflict a heavy burden on the environment. Building materials like steel beams, vinyl siding, bricks, wooden planks and concrete require significant amounts of energy to fabricate. Dark external finishes absorb heat. Synthetic fabrics used in indoor carpeting and furniture coverings give off fumes that can diminish air quality and lead to respiratory illnesses. "Closed" buildings, with sealed windows, also tend to be either overheated or overcooled.

Some architects began experimenting with eco-buildings in the 1960s, but green design only caught on seriously in Europe in the mid-1990s, when the EU enacted minimum energy efficiency standards for new buildings. In the US and Canada, environmental design remains largely voluntary, although in some cities, like Vancouver and Toronto, local planning policies provide developers and government agencies with incentives to erect green buildings or complete energy retrofits on existing ones. As well, North American builders can have their projects "LEED certified" — meaning the final structures are rated according to five design criteria by local chapters of the Green Buildings Council, which created the Leadership in Environmental and Energy Design designation in 1993. (The LEED program has been criticized as overly restrictive and time-consuming.)

Sustainable buildings have many characteristics. They may

use recycled building materials or choose alternative designs to minimize the use of certain components. (Renowned British architect Norman Foster developed a crosshatch pattern for the beams that hold up his office towers because it requires less steel.) The buildings are oriented to take advantage of the sun's heat. Insulation goes well beyond building code minimums. Windows are double or triple glazed to prevent heat loss, and there is an emphasis on allowing in natural light and air to reduce the need for electricity. Some green buildings also use geothermal systems for heating, and others will find ways of collecting and recycling rainwater, for example, to water a green roof or a garden.

Location, however, is a key feature of any green building. In cities like Rotterdam, some of the best examples of eco-architecture can be found on derelict land near the port, which is being redeveloped with sustainable housing.[32] By choosing to build on vacant urban land accessible by transit and well served by municipal infrastructure, developers are heeding the first of the three Rs: re-use (the other two are reduce and recycle).

The point is that cities can do all sorts of things to mitigate their impact on the environment, but none are as important as the way they manage the transportation infrastructure that serves as the circulation system of every urban region.

Chapter 5
Cities and Transportation

In the developed world, cities are increasingly planned around the space and energy demands of cars and trucks. In the developing world, meanwhile, megacities are overwhelmed by congestion and air pollution as huge numbers of vehicles crowd into historic urban cores that can't accommodate the traffic. Rather than allowing city-dwellers to go about their day-to-day business, vehicle-clogged roads and highways inhibit the way people function in cities — a crisis that threatens the economic, social and environmental well-being of the urban regions that now house the majority of the world's inhabitants.

Car-oriented planning saps the energy of urban spaces:
• In small and mid-sized urban centers, the proliferation of large-format malls, big-box stores and highways drains business from vibrant downtowns, with their pedestrian-oriented retail strips, public buildings, restaurants and theaters. Malls can't replicate the vitality and convenience of urban cores. Disconnected from adjoining neighborhoods, they are inaccessible by foot or bicycle, and dominated by chains.
• Driving is an isolating experience, whereas taking transit, cycling or walking through urban neighborhoods are inherently social activities that connect city-dwellers to one another. Moreover, driving can be stressful: road rage has become

endemic in large cities and some health studies point to a link between heart attacks and commuting on busy highways.

• Cars are deadlier than firearms. In the US, about 43,000 people die in vehicle collisions each year,[1] compared with about 30,000 gun-related deaths.[2]

• Over time, streets, highways and rights-of-way have grown to accommodate more and larger vehicles. The road network takes up as much as 35 percent of available space in North American metropolitan regions, compared with 20 to 25 percent in older European cities and 10 to 12 percent in Asian centers.[3]

Since the 1960s, urbanists and environmentalists have issued warnings about the escalating problems associated with car-oriented planning. The solutions include transit, pedestrian and cycling-friendly planning and policy; financial disincentives to driving; and a fundamental shift in attitudes about the impact cars and light trucks have on the urban environment. But while some countries and jurisdictions have embraced these and other solutions, many cities resist change or are simply unable to muster the resources needed to meaningfully alter car-oriented growth patterns.

Land-use Planning and Sustainable Transportation

Car-dependent cities, like Houston, Calgary and Atlanta, tend to be very spread out geographically. They are also not conducive to transit service, and therefore they have very low transit ridership. Most people drive when they need to get somewhere.

The reason is that there's a powerful economic relationship between transit, population density and land-use planning. Transit agencies must make substantial investments in vehicles

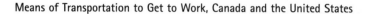

Means of Transportation to Get to Work, Canada and the United States

Means of Transportation	% trips taken	Canada United States

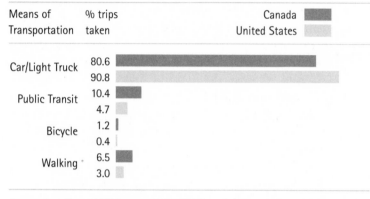

Car/Light Truck	80.6 90.8	
Public Transit	10.4 4.7	
Bicycle	1.2 0.4	
Walking	6.5 3.0	

Source: Canadian and US Censuses, 2000, 2001[4]

and other equipment, like signaling systems. They have hefty operating expenses, such as drivers' salaries, vehicle maintenance and fuel costs. Most transit agencies receive some form of subsidy from local or regional governments, but they must also recover a significant portion of their costs from fares and other forms of revenue, such as advertising. So without a critical mass of riders, transit service becomes unaffordable and inefficient. In general, transit riders want convenience, reliable and efficient service, and value for their money. When a transit service doesn't generate enough revenue, it often cuts back on service — for example, by reducing the number of vehicles running on a given route. And when that happens, commuters with a choice of transportation modes are much more likely to rely on their vehicles than on transit.

Transit and planning experts know that in sprawling, low-density suburban areas, there simply are not enough residents to create the pool of potential customers needed to make transit service convenient and frequent; the economies of scale aren't present. Studies of Canadian cities, for example, show that the farther people live from their places of work, the less likely they are to use transit.[5]

Yet there's more to the transit-land use relationship than just population density. Transit stops must be conveniently located (within five to ten minutes' walking distance of homes and apartments, or in the case of commuter rail service, equipped with park-and-ride lots). And they have to take riders to the places they want to go, which generally means areas with a high concentration of offices, shops, and cultural or sports venues. While this may sound obvious, the history of higher order transit (subways, light-rail lines, streetcars) is littered with examples of the proverbial tail wagging the dog. Eager to score political points and cut ribbons, local politicians sometimes press ahead with pricey transit schemes, hoping that if they build, the riders will come. But then they don't.

Indeed, subway or light-rail projects risk becoming white elephants unless they've been carefully integrated into land-use planning policies that direct medium- and high-density development (e.g., office or apartment towers) into the areas that will be served by these transit lines. Effective transit service tends to function on the so-called hub-and-spoke model: most transit riders use the service to travel to their workplaces,[6] so land-use policies must encourage office developers and other commercial developers to invest in core areas with easy access to subway, streetcar and commuter rail stations.

Large cities with successful transit systems — such as Tokyo, where annual subway ridership exceeds 2.6 billion rides — have

Japan's High-Speed Trains

As part of the preparations for the 1964 Summer Olympics, Japan launched the world's first high-speed commuter rail network, known as Shinkansen. Since then, these Japanese bullet trains, which can travel at speeds exceeding 300 kilometers per hour (186 miles per hour), have revolutionized travel within the country. The major urban centers are all linked by these remarkable vehicles. In 2004, its fortieth anniversary, the Shinkansen rail network (now privatized), extended almost 2,500 kilometers (1,553 miles), and had carried an estimated 4.6 billion passengers. Several new lines are under construction or in the planning stages.

There can be little doubt about the environmental benefits of the Japanese bullet trains in terms of reduced greenhouse gas emissions, both from cars and air travel. In a country dependent on imported oil and gas, it makes economic sense for commuters to travel by train. But because of the service's speed and efficiency (most Shinkansen trains pull into the station literally within seconds of their scheduled arrival times), Japanese commuters don't have to be persuaded to use them when traveling between cities like Tokyo and Osaka.

Outside Japan, the best-known high-speed trains operate in France, Germany, South Korea and Taiwan, but several other countries are building or planning similar lines, including China, Spain and Italy.[7] The state of California is also considering a high-speed service between Los Angeles, San Francisco and Sacramento.[8]

recognized the importance of integrating the various modes — buses, subways, streetcars, commuter rail (see Japan's High-Speed Trains) — into a seamless network where the emphasis is on convenience and efficient service. This means riders can easily switch from one service to another at multimodal transit stations, as well as travel using a single fare or pass card.

Perhaps the most crucial ingredient in building transit-friendly cities is the regional perspective. Metropolitan areas often encompass numerous municipalities. They are home to multiple transit operators and are crisscrossed by urban highways, major bridges, commuter rail lines and arterial roads. The residents, in turn, travel throughout such regions with little regard to internal municipal borders. They may rely on cars for some trips and transit or a combination of both for others. Consequently, large urban areas need public agencies or authorities with a mandate to oversee the integration of land-use planning and transportation across the entire region. In Greater New York, the Metropolitan Transportation Authority operates subways, buses and regional commuter trains that serve the regions beyond the city borders. In Vancouver, an agency called TransLink was established in 1999 to plan transit service, major road improvements and cycling infrastructure throughout Greater Vancouver. Ultimately, the goal is to encourage "transit-oriented development" — dense, pedestrian-friendly cities with plenty of vitality and a reduced dependence on the automobile.

The Rise and Fall of the Inner-city Highway

In the 1950s and 1960s, many growth-minded cities approved ambitious highway building schemes designed to revitalize downtowns and relieve traffic congestion. These involved bulldozing slums or scruffy working-class neighborhoods to make way for broad freeways — some elevated, others below grade — that would allow the middle-class residents of fast-growing bedroom suburbs to commute into downtown business districts. New York writer Jane Jacobs led a fierce grassroots fight to stop a freeway planned to cut through Greenwich Village, and her spirited opposition quickly spread to other cities, including San Francisco, Portland, Toronto and Vancouver. While activists succeeded in blocking some of these ambitious road-building schemes, many cities allowed such projects to proceed, leaving a legacy of carved-up downtowns.

Over time, the failings of inner-city highways have become difficult to ignore. Rather than expediting car travel, they concentrate traffic and become mired in gridlock. In terms of their surroundings, highways are nearly insurmountable barriers, physically dividing the communities through which they pass. Nor are they good neighbors: they cast off fumes, noise and salt, as well as pump traffic into crowded downtown areas. Lastly, politicians know that postwar urban highways haven't aged gracefully: the constant pounding of traffic creates fractures and potholes, and it may even cause whole sections of overpasses or bridges to collapse, with tragic consequences, as happened in Montreal in 2006 and Minneapolis in 2007.

Transit-oriented Development[9]

• Within a five- to ten-minute walk of transit stops
• A mix of land uses — employment, retail, institutional, residential, recreational — that allows the area to be in use around the clock, and served by 24/7 transit lines
• Vibrant urban design and "memorable" public spaces
• Small blocks to encourage circulation and traffic dispersal
• No minimum parking rules, meaning that office and apartment developers aren't compelled to provide spaces for every user
• Planning policies that discourage surface parking lots and cheap parking
• Traffic calming
• Cycling infrastructure, such as bike lanes and bike posts

Over the years, architects and developers have put forward various ideas for mitigating the impact of inner-city highways, such as hiving off lanes for express bus routes. Some urbanists have advocated demolishing these expressways, arguing that traffic will simply dissipate as drivers find alternative routes. In

San Francisco, a 1989 earthquake destroyed the elevated Embarcadero Expressway, and city officials, in a bold move, decided not to rebuild it. Instead, the path of the expressway, long a derelict strip in the shadow of a busy highway, was revitalized, allowing improved connections between the downtown and the city's waterfront wharf areas. Boston, for its part, buried its highly congested waterfront expressway, known as the Central Artery, in a $14.6 billion project dubbed "The Big Dig" that took fifteen years to complete. Although the project was nearly crippled by cost overruns, accidents and scandals, it created 100 hectares (250 acres) of new space near Boston's waterfront.[10]

But demolition isn't the only solution to the problems created by urban highways. Since the 1980s, a network of London-based not-for-profit community groups has reclaimed 8 hectares (20 acres) of unused land beneath the Westway, an elevated highway that slices through dense working-class neighborhoods in the northwest of the British city. These groups have built sports fields, playgrounds, childcare centers, commercial buildings and live-work artist studios beneath the expressway. In this way, they've integrated the region underneath the highway into the community.[11]

Road Pricing and Congestion Charges

In wealthy nations, where the rate of car ownership is high, one of the major causes of traffic congestion is that individuals don't pay the full price of driving their vehicles. At first, this may seem like a counterintuitive statement. After all, in order to drive, one pays for the car, as well as auto insurance premiums, fuel, maintenance and various licensing fees. Indeed, the cost of driving is high and rising.

But in most cities, such outlays don't begin to cover all the costs associated with operating a vehicle. Individuals don't pay directly for their use of the roads, in the way that a cell phone customer is billed for each second of connect time. Rather, most municipalities finance road maintenance and construction through property tax revenue. The result, however, is that those who don't do much driving effectively subsidize those who use their car for every journey. It's the same in areas where highways are "free," meaning drivers don't pay tolls.

On the other hand, commuters must buy tickets if they wish to travel on transit; in other words, the fare is a user fee, and the amount one pays is closely related to the amount one travels. Transit agencies depend on a combination of government subsidies and fare revenues to finance their operations — paying salaries, buying transit vehicles, building new lines. But the bottom line for the consumer is that the service isn't free.

There's no such pricing system for cars, even though municipal governments spend enormous sums to build, maintain, police and repair urban roads and highways. Yet when one gets in one's car and drives, no money changes hands. The effect is that drivers are shielded from the full cost of using their vehicles, which encourages overuse. There's little economic disincentive beyond the price of gas.

In fact, there are other hidden subsidies for drivers. In suburban areas, many companies have large surface parking lots that can be used for free by shoppers or employees. The parking lots are not, in fact, free – it costs money to build and maintain them. Often the property owners are allowed to deduct such expenses from their taxes. In other words, the tax system indirectly subsidizes drivers.

As traffic congestion worsens, there has been mounting

interest in "road pricing" policies that ensure drivers pay more of the cost of using their vehicles. These include tolls on highways, ring roads, bridges and tunnels; gas and carbon taxes; and hefty parking levies on spaces in busy downtown areas, where land is scarce and traffic is heavy. While highway tolls aren't new, more and more jurisdictions have been moving to implement various road-pricing systems since the mid-1990s. Transportation economists regard such measures as a more effective way of financing this kind of infrastructure.

Some forms of road pricing are explicitly designed to discourage car ownership and/or usage as a means of reducing air pollution and congestion. In Singapore, for example, the government's various vehicle ownership and parking fees are so high — over $100,000 — that driving becomes financially punishing for all but the most affluent. While Singapore's approach reflects that nation's space constraints and its autocratic form of government, other large cities have begun to experiment with so-called congestion pricing as a means of discouraging car use downtown. The best-known example is London. In 2003, former mayor Ken Livingstone imposed a congestion charge to raise revenue for transit, with initial projections of £1.3 billion ($2.5 billion) over the first ten years. The charge, which is in effect from 7 a.m. to 6:30 p.m., also created a financial disincentive for driving into a 21-square-kilometer (8-square-mile) swath of the city's core, characterized by a haphazard street pattern and extremely slow-moving traffic.

The results, observed traffic expert Derek Turner, "are impressive. Journey times to, from, and across the priced zone are down by 14%. Time spent stationary or traveling at less than 10 kilometers per hour is down by 25%. Benefits are evident on the public transport side as well, with excess bus waiting times for routes serving the charge zone down by 33%. And in a side benefit that few made specific mention of early on, we are seeing fewer road accidents."[12]

Other jurisdictions are following London's lead. In 2006, Sweden established a congestion charge for Stockholm, levied electronically at all the entrance points into the city. A year later, New York mayor Michael Bloomberg announced plans (later blocked by the state) to establish a congestion charge in Manhattan, and other cities looking to reduce their greenhouse gas emissions are following suit.

These moves are not without controversy: in London, some small downtown businesses have been negatively affected by the congestion charge. Despite that, the city is expanding the limits. Voters in the Stockholm region rejected a six-month trial of the congestion fee system during a 2006 referendum, but the national government overruled the result and imposed it as a tax, with the proceeds going into transit improvements.[13]

The Future of Subways and Light Rail

Many of the world's great metropolitan subway/rail systems were conceived and built in an era very different from ours. In the late nineteenth century and the early decades of the twentieth century, most large cities had extensive streetcar networks and much inter-city travel took place along busy passenger rail lines. Subways represented the logical next step in transportation technology. In the postwar era, rapidly expanding cities throughout Japan invested steadily, and heavily, in fully integrated transit networks designed to accommodate dense urban neighborhoods. Cities in the former Soviet Bloc — such as Moscow and Prague — built efficient rapid transit systems to serve the needs of the urban working class. Meanwhile, North

Asian and Middle Eastern Cities with Rapid Transit Systems Built Since the 1990s

City	Number of Stations	Length
Guangzhou, China (1999)	60	116 km
Shanghai, China (1995)	162	230 km
Shenzhen, China (2004)	19	22 km
Delhi, India (2002)	59	65 km
Tehran, Iran (2000)	40	48 km
Kuala Lumpur, Malaysia (1996, 1998)	49	56 km
Bangkok, Thailand (1999, 2004)	41	44 km

Source: Wikipedia, http://en.wikipedia.org/wiki/List_of_rapid_transit_systems.

American cities like San Francisco/Oakland and Greater Toronto established regional commuter rail networks aimed at the burgeoning population of bedroom communities fanning out from the traditional downtown.

In recent decades, large Asian cities experiencing robust economic growth have been building new metro and commuter rail networks, while many more are planned or under construction in Dublin and Tel Aviv, Hanoi and Dubai. In the economically robust Chilean capital of Santiago, meanwhile, the subway system has been in expansion mode since the late 1990s, partly to deal with crowding on privately operated bus routes, but also as a means of extending service out to the recently developed modern suburbs on the city's periphery.

Indeed, the global pace of rapid transit construction has been accelerating since the 1980s, largely due to the urbanization of the developing world. But in wealthier countries, the combination of automobile ownership and postwar suburban sprawl have worked against rapid transit. Suburban distances and densities are not conducive to subways, which are extremely expensive to build and operate. Cities like Madrid (see Madrid's Subway Building Spree), have continued to make significant expansions to existing rapid transit networks, but many more make incremental changes by extending lines. One reason: new downtown lines — for example, New York City's proposed Second Avenue subway — come with enormous price tags. In cities like London and Greater Vancouver, governments have had to set up public-private partnerships to finance and operate rapid transit systems.

An older transportation technology — light-rail vehicles or streetcars operating in their own rights-of-way — is a cost-effective alternative to traditional subways. Streetcars (or trams) have been a fixture in many European, Russian and Japanese cities for decades, but many were phased out in North America during the postwar era in favor of electric trolleys and diesel buses. But in Toronto during the 1980s, pro-streetcar activists persuaded the city's transit agency not to mothball its streetcar fleet. Since then, streetcars have been redesigned: the newest models are longer and sleeker, and new streetcar routes are being built across the city. Today, dozens of US cities, using federal and state funding, are rushing to deploy new streetcar systems to help alleviate traffic congestion.

Bus Rapid Transit

The notion of creating dedicated surface transit corridors isn't just limited to light-rail systems. Bus rapid-transit (BRT) networks, which date back to the 1960s, allow municipal buses to operate on an exclusive highway or street lane, or along purpose-built "busways." In North America, a growing number of cities have created so-called high-occupancy-vehicle lanes to accommodate buses, as well as private vehicles with more than two passengers. Some municipal transit agencies offer express bus service along major arterial roads, which also have priority signals that allow the buses to move more quickly through traffic. But in true BRT systems, there are lanes or tunnels reserved exclusively for buses.

Ottawa is home to one of the oldest and best-used BRT systems, but several other large North American cities have such lines, including Los Angeles, Denver, Boston, Pittsburgh and Minneapolis-St. Paul.[15] BRT is also popular in major Australian cities and some Asian capitals, such as Taipei and Bangkok.

Much of the development of new BRT networks is taking place in large metropolitan regions in South America, Asia and Africa. In some cases, governments are using BRT projects to achieve multiple transportation goals. In the Chinese city of Guangzhou, with 10 million inhabitants, the construction of a 23-kilometer-long (14-mile-long) BRT has coincided with a gradual push to eliminate motorcycles from the city core. Officials want to tackle the problem of motorcyclists driving on sidewalks among pedestrians, and the ban has prompted an increase in cycling and transit use.[16] Meanwhile, in Johannesburg in 2006, city officials, using financial support provided by Bill Clinton's climate change fund, began construction on a 94-kilometer (58-mile) BRT network in preparation for the 2010 soccer World Cup. With this system, municipal leaders are looking for ways to allow privately owned minibus taxis to share the new BRT network. Under apartheid, minibuses were one of the few industries open to blacks. With the development of the BRT network, the city wants these semilegal firms to formalize themselves and compete on a level playing field with the municipal bus companies.[17]

The Cycling Revolution

For years, cycling was a popular and well-established form of urban transportation in countries such as Denmark, Germany, the Netherlands and China. After a visit to Beijing in the 1970s, former New York mayor Ed Koch was so taken by the sight of thousands of cyclists that he ordered the construction of segregated bike lanes along some of the Big Apple's major thoroughfares. He wasn't alone. At the time, municipal officials in Ottawa and Toronto were beginning to consider establishing urban bike paths to serve the growing number of recreational cycling enthusiasts. But some also saw bike paths as a way to reduce congestion and air pollution by providing residents with an alternative means of getting to work.

The cycling revolution encountered many potholes before local politicians began to think seriously about the true potential of bike networks. Soon after they had been constructed, Koch tore up NYC's bike lanes, claiming they weren't being used.[18] In 1981, the City of Ottawa cancelled funding for a five-year plan to build a 309-kilometer (192-mile) network of bike lanes and paths,[19] while other metropolitan regions paid little more than lip service to the need to improve cycling routes.

Almost three decades later, urban cycling has become a much more mainstream part of the debate about how to make cities less congested, healthier and more sustainable. But as those early false starts suggest, it was not an easy journey. In car-oriented cities, transportation planners, commuters and many local politicians began from the premise that the roads were for cars, motorcycles, trucks and transit vehicles.

Cycling activists argued that drivers shouldn't assume they have exclusive use of the roads. Some municipalities proposed — and built — bike paths through parks and, occasionally, on their own rights-of-way. But cycling advocates pushed for the establishment of bike lanes on major streets.

Such moves may involve a reduction in the number of lanes available to drivers, and so the provision of bike lanes has been controversial. But as traffic congestion becomes ever more severe, a growing number of cities have invested in bike lane networks, with promises of more to come. Some are a lane delineated by a painted median and run parallel to traffic.

Some cities have made other key changes designed to promote cycling, such as installing thousands of O-ring posts (in Toronto) or full-scale bike parking lots (as in Japan) so riders don't have difficulty finding places to leave their bikes. And as it has become easier to ride to work, some employers are also providing changing rooms with showers and indoor bike parking for employees who are cyclists.

In 2007 Paris radically raised the profile of urban cycling with the introduction of Vélib', a low-cost bike rental service devised by Mayor Bertrand Delanoë, a long-time green activist. After winning office in 2001, he began to reduce car lanes in favor of about 200 kilometers (124 miles) of new on-street bike paths. His next move was striking a deal with a French outdoor advertising agency to underwrite the rental operation. Using electronic locks and self-serve pay kiosks, bikes are stored at hundreds of "stations" and riders can rent them using bank cards for as little as one Euro ($1.55) per day. The city initially deployed 10,600 bikes, but it quickly doubled the size of the fleet due to Vélib''s enormous popularity with both tourists and Parisians.[20] (Other cities — Lyons and Montreal — are following suit.)

Safety, however, remains a stubborn impediment for the urban cycling movement, particularly in cities where drivers aren't used to sharing the road with bikes. Even with helmets and other safety gear, cyclists run a considerable risk of being hurt or killed in collisions with vehicles. They can be blind-sided by turning cars or "doored." Reckless cyclists or bicycle couriers also pose a threat to pedestrians when they use side-walks or race through busy intersections.

The risk factors are linked to the provision of cycling infra-structure. As Paris's experience suggests, when a critical mass of cyclists takes to the road, the accident rate drops. The city's cycling officials say that the number of bikes on the streets increased 50 percent between 2001 and 2007, but there has been no increase in the number of accidents.

Green Vehicles

Since Toyota introduced the Prius, in 1997, consumers have bought more than a million hybrid vehicles, which rely on a technology that allows the motor to switch between a battery-

Biking in Bogotá

When Enrique Peñalosa was elected mayor of Bogotá in 1998, the Colombian cap-ital had grown into a crowded metropolis of 7 million that was seen as a haven for thousands of refugees fleeing the country's drug-related civil war. "We decid-ed to make the city more for children than for cars," Peñalosa recalled several years later, explaining Bogotá's sudden transformation into one of the world's great biking cities.[21]

In short order, Peñalosa banned parking on sidewalks and expanded the city's transit system. But his masterstroke was the establishment of a 300-kilometer (186-mile) network of bike lanes and paths known as "ciclo-rutas." He decreed that for seven hours each Sunday, 120 kilometers (75 miles) of the city's arterial roads would be car-free. These moves triggered an amazing increase in biking in the city. According to the New York–based Institute for Transportation and Development Policy, the proportion of the population that cycles jumped tenfold between 1997 and 2001, from 0.5 percent to 5 percent.

powered engine and a traditional combustion version. Hybrids and other compact cars are more energy-efficient, and thus less harmful to the atmosphere.

There's little consensus about the future of hybrids. In California cities such as San Francisco/Oakland, hybrids are widely used. Some observers say the market can only expand as fuel prices skyrocket, while others feel that hybrids will remain a niche vehicle, geared to environmentally conscious consumers.

Quite apart from such broad consumer trends, a growing number of municipalities have adopted various clean vehicle technologies in order to cut emissions. These include hybrid cab fleets and city buses that run on biodiesel fuel (which is refined from waste oils, animal fats and other organics). Some transit agencies and courier companies are experimenting with vehicles that use engines powered by hydrogen fuel cells — engines linked to batteries that generate electricity by combining hydrogen and oxygen. In California and British Columbia, governments underwrote such efforts by helping to finance networks of hydrogen refueling stations. Researchers will also be trying to incorporate solar cells into vehicle design with an eye to augmenting traditional engines with technologies that use low-emission renewable energy to power vehicles.

There's little question that the future of these technologies turns on their acceptance in large metropolitan regions, with their economies of scale. That's why environmentally conscious municipalities are pushing to convert their various fleets — taxis, city trucks, transit vehicles — to these more sustainable technologies. With their collective purchasing power, large municipalities have the ability to expand the market for such vehicles, and thus drive down the prices for consumers.

Chapter 6
Urban Poverty

Poverty has always been a fact of city life. In ancient Rome and Athens, the majesty of the temples and public buildings stood in sharp contrast to residential areas where the inhabitants lived in squalid conditions. Two millennia later, Britain's raw Industrial Age cities witnessed the growth of fetid working-class slums, as well as debtors' prisons for those who couldn't pay their bills (the practice was made illegal after 1869). In fact, the word "slum" emerged from nineteenth-century England, coined to describe overcrowded industrial areas with run-down housing occupied by the poor.

In our era, globalization has widened the gap between the richest and poorest inhabitants of outwardly robust cities characterized by thriving business districts, lively downtowns and a steady stream of business travelers and tourists.

However, poverty is a relative term. A minimum wage salary in Canada or Australia may be equivalent to a small fortune in a poor country. An apartment considered to be cramped and run-down by Seattle standards may seem spacious and well-equipped to a family that has just immigrated from one of Manila's shanty towns.

But such comparisons are of limited value. Rather, the more important gradients of urban wealth and poverty can be found within the context of an individual city. To truly under-stand urban poverty, one must ask certain questions: What is the degree of income disparity within a particular city? Is there an adequate supply of affordable housing? Are the poor physi-cally and socially isolated from the urban mainstream, or do low-income neighborhoods have access to the sorts of civic amenities available to more affluent communities? Lastly, do cities seek to build mixed-income communities or do they iso-late the poor in ghettos and the affluent in enclaves?

For well over a century, reformers in North American and European cities have struggled to ameliorate urban poverty. The labor movement sought to organize workers, many of them poor immigrants, who toiled in factories in rapidly grow-ing industrial cities. Social activists created day nursery pro-grams for working parents while ethno-cultural groups set up housing/resettlement agencies to help newcomers establish themselves in crowded cities. By the postwar era, when mem-ories of the hardships of the Great Depression were still vivid, many governments in the West created social safety nets, such as medical insurance, old age security, unemployment insur-ance, social housing programs, and welfare/disability benefits. These policies weren't targeted at city-dwellers per se, but they had the effect of reducing urban poverty.

Yet some cities have also sought to sweep away the physical evidence of poverty, for example, by clearing slums in the name of public health, or to make way for highways and large housing projects. More recently, some big-city politicians have pursued aggressive campaigns to remove homeless individuals from city streets in the name of improving public safety and promoting tourism.

Meanwhile, in developing world megacities such as Mumbai

and Beijing, local and national officials have undertaken large-scale slum clearance campaigns that displace hundreds of thousands of residents so that desirable urban land can be redeveloped.

In fact, one of the fundamental challenges associated with urban poverty — in wealthy and developing nations alike — is the provision of adequate housing for city-dwellers. While few question the importance of something as basic as decent shelter, the problem of how to provide sufficient housing for urban populations is fraught with complexity.

Social housing has been a political hot potato in some affluent countries for decades. But as the developing world becomes increasingly urbanized, the sheer magnitude of the problem grows ever more overwhelming. With 70 million people leaving rural areas and settling in cities each year, the world's cities "must build 35 million homes a year," observes journalist Robert Neuwirth, who writes about life in the slums and shanty towns of the developing world. "That's 96,150 a day, 4,000 homes an hour, 66 homes a minute... And this would only maintain the equilibrium. It would not house the billion who are living as squatters today." The United Nations estimates that by 2020, the world's cities need to construct homes for 670 million people, a $300-billion undertaking.[1]

Being Poor and Urban

Wealth, talent and resources are not distributed equitably within society. In most nations, rural communities tend to be less affluent and more economically vulnerable than cities. That disparity is a driver of urbanization: cities, on balance, offer more opportunity. Despite that, urban poverty persists alongside urban economic success, social programs and other measures intended to alleviate hardship.

The face of urban poverty is as diverse as the city itself. The ranks of the poor may encompass members of minority groups who've been subjected to racial discrimination, single-parent families, seniors on fixed incomes, individuals with disabilities or mental illness, welfare recipients, blue-collar workers who've seen their jobs disappear with factory closings, and recent immigrants unable to find well-paying jobs because they lack language skills or legal documents. In many global cities, there are also growing numbers of the so-called working poor — families or individuals who hold down multiple low-paying jobs yet continue to tread water financially due to the high cost of urban living (see Janitors for Justice).

Within affluent cities, poverty may be visible or hidden. The more obvious signs of poverty include homeless people sleeping on the streets, shelters, soup kitchens, drop-in centers, public housing complexes and food banks. Low-income families tend to congregate in areas with an abundance of low-rent apartments and rooming houses. Yet they may also be forced to live in temporary housing, cheap hotels, bed-and-breakfasts or basement suites in middle-class or mixed-income neighborhoods where class distinctions aren't as readily apparent.

In some cities, outward signs of poverty — such as homelessness or the demand for shelter beds — merely hint at deeper issues. Calgary and Edmonton, in the throes of Alberta's oil sands boom, have seen housing prices soar. People from across Canada and elsewhere flock to these urban centers to take advantage of the prosperity and the abundance of work. As a result, both cities have experienced severe housing shortages, which means that many newcomers have found jobs but can't secure a decent place to live.

Housing markets and location, in fact, play an important

Janitors for Justice

Early in the twentieth century, the North American labor movement took root in large cities filled with recent immigrants who toiled under abysmal conditions in factories, producing everything from garments to steel to cars. Since the 1970s, however, the union movement has struggled to expand in the manufacturing sector as firms move their production facilities to nonunion jurisdictions or low-wage countries.

But the urban labor movement has witnessed a resurgence as it has focused attention on the fast-growing service sectors that exist in thriving global cities. In the mid-1980s, for example, thousands of janitors working nights in office buildings in Denver and Los Angeles decided they'd had enough. A workforce dominated by visible minorities and immigrants, janitors toiled for paltry wages and no benefits. In Houston, 5,300 janitors earned as little as $100 a week.[2]

In 1986, the Service Employees International Union (SEIU) launched ambitious organizing campaigns in several major US cities, first recruiting thousands of janitors, and later, low-wage employees working in convention centers and the hospitality sector. The SEIU estimates it recruited 80 percent of janitors in target cities.

Today, the so-called Janitors for Justice movement is 225,000 strong, and operates in urban centers across the US. The union has succeeded in negotiating better wages and benefit packages that have helped lift many janitors out of poverty.[3]

A similar organizing drive has targeted the big city hotel sector. UNITE HERE — a 450,000-member union representing workers in needle trades and hotels and restaurants — has been successful in pushing international hotel chains such as Hilton to improve difficult working conditions for maids and cleaning staff in cities like Atlanta, Toronto and San Francisco.[4]

Both movements recognize that fast-growing North American cities have large minority/immigrant workforces that serve the needs of the international business class. Because the economies of global cities are so dependent on office towers filled with financial services firms, five-star hotels and conventional facilities, SEIU and UNITE HERE were able to use the threat of strikes and strategic bargaining to support these workers.

role in perpetuating or even exacerbating poverty. In working-class or low-income communities on the upswing, rents may become increasingly unaffordable. Meanwhile, residents of areas perceived to be poor and/or dangerous may have difficulty finding work simply because of where they live. Such neighborhoods can also be physically isolated from the urban mainstream, forcing those with jobs to travel long distances to workplaces. At the same time, low-income areas tend to lack jobs, thus contributing to employment shortages.

Ironically, the relative cost of living in low-income neighborhoods can be surprisingly high. Catering to a segment of the population that lacks clout, slum landlords are able to charge hefty rents that soak up a significant portion of a tenant's income. Meanwhile, supermarkets may avoid establishing outlets in poor neighborhoods, forcing residents to purchase staples at marked-up prices in convenience stores.

The most notorious version of this practice is known as "redlining." From the 1930s to the late 1960s, US banks, insurance companies and federal financial institutions drew red lines around minority neighborhoods on maps of cities like Philadelphia. Citing financial risk, these institutions refused to write loans or policies to the residents of redlined areas; many were African Americans. Redlining has been implicated in the decline of many inner cities in the US. It was made illegal in 1968 with the passage of the *Fair Housing Act*.[5]

Affordable Housing

In many households, the cost of shelter (rent, mortgage payments, maintenance, utilities) represents the largest single expense. Yet in spite of its cost, housing is also a basic human need, like food and water. This dichotomy helps explain why urban poverty is so closely linked to the supply of affordable housing within a given city. If the supply is limited and demand is high, housing prices and rents tend to rise — it's simple economics. For individuals or families with limited

Gentrification and Poverty

Since the 1960s, gentrification has become a familiar fixture of urban regeneration in many large cities, as run-down homes in older, working-class or low-income neighborhoods are bought by young families and renovated, thereby increasing property values. In some areas, gentrification is part of the natural cycle of cities – one generation of owners grows old and moves out, allowing the next group to come in. But in other districts, gentrification can lead to a reduction in the supply of affordable urban housing and an increase in the cost of living.

It works like this: in older working-class neighborhoods that may have fallen on hard times, single-family homes are carved up and turned into rooming houses or group homes, with cheap rents. The tenants may include students, poor families, welfare recipients and people with physical or mental disabilities. Then the pendulum begins to swing the other way. Perhaps the area is discovered by artists looking for apartments where they can also have a studio. Or the neighborhood's housing stock has some historic character and is desirable for renovators. Gradually, as more affluent buyers come into these areas, the rooming houses are bought up and converted back into single-family dwellings. Tenants are evicted and forced to find accommodation elsewhere. The growing desirability brings higher rents, which erode the standard of living of low-income city-dwellers.

Gentrification can lead to a 180-degree shift in the socio-economic profile of a neighborhood, leaving a diminished stock of affordable housing. But some cities have devised ways of breaking this dynamic. In Amsterdam, for example, a not-for-profit community housing organization buys up derelict buildings in older neighborhoods and renovates them into low-rise apartment complexes geared to low-income tenants. The quality of the restoration work is so high, says urban heritage expert Anthony Tung, that these projects will trigger the regeneration of a run-down neighborhood.

income, the result can be deepening poverty: as housing consumes an ever larger portion of the weekly paycheck, there's less left over for clothing, education, health care, transportation, even food.

The history of government involvement in urban housing dates back to the late nineteenth century, when municipal agencies began cleaning up slums and building modern sanitation systems to reduce the threat of infectious disease. By the 1920s, governments started taking an even more active role, with the development of social housing. The movement has its roots in Europe in the pre-World War II period, but eventually spread to North America, Australia, the United Kingdom and city-states like Hong Kong and Singapore.

From the late 1940s onward, many large cities built extensive public housing complexes. In Europe, subsidized housing developments weren't necessarily reserved for the poor; in countries like Sweden, Austria and France, the proportion of families living in public housing is large by North American standards.

But in the US, UK and Canada, the provision of subsidized housing was regarded as a postwar social program as well as an instrument of urban renewal. In some cases, local councils and housing agencies would buy up unused real estate for new housing projects. In others, municipalities would expropriate and demolish tenements or homes in older neighborhoods perceived to be in decline, then redevelop the land with large apartment blocks.

In large British cities, such as London and Manchester, council housing is a familiar feature of the urban landscape, despite continuing pressure since the 1980s to privatize units by selling these "estates" to tenants or housing associations.

Today, there are an estimated 3 million council-housing tenants in Britain and another 1.6 million on waiting lists. (Prime Minister Gordon Brown's Labor government said in 2007 that it plans to spend £8 billion ($15.7 billion) by 2011 to increase the number of affordable rental units in Britain by 50 percent.[6])

In major American cities, by contrast, the public housing story has been mired in controversy and tragedy rather than proactive policy-making. The development of massive public housing projects in the 1960s created impoverished racial ghettos followed by a political backlash against subsidized housing. On Chicago's South Side, for example, a thriving African-American community, known as Bronzeville, was razed in favor of a long row of sixteen-storey high rises called the Robert Taylor Homes. By the time they were finally demolished in 2006, the notorious Robert Taylor Homes had become synonymous with crime, drugs and violence. As was the case with many large-scale public housing projects, those with means moved out, leaving behind a concentration of residents who were unemployed or on welfare. Similar conditions exist in some of Paris's *banlieue*, or suburbs — subsidized high rises populated by disaffected migrant laborers who rioted for several weeks during the fall of 2005.

In the wake of the social disaster created by the first wave of North American public housing, more sensitive approaches emerged, including grants and incentives designed to encourage the development of co-op housing, not-for-profit housing and small-scale public housing — that is, townhouse or small apartment complexes rather than towering apartment blocks. There's also an increased emphasis on combining subsidized and so-called market housing within the same development to reduce the social tensions created by concentrating poverty.

Yet, as the UK government has acknowledged with its new long-range housing strategy, the case in favor of social housing remains rooted in the failure of the private market to keep up with demand in rapidly growing urban areas. In the global cities of the twenty-first century, affordable housing must remain a critical tool for governments determined to reduce the income gap between the rich and the urban underclass.

Poverty and Housing in Squatter Cities

The affordable housing issues confronting the wealthy cities of the North bear scant resemblance to the social crises that exist in the dense, impoverished slums of Africa, Asia and, to a lesser extent, Latin America (see Slum Growth).

According to the United Nations Secretariat for Human Settlements (UN Habitat) report, *The State of the World's Cities*

Slum Growth

One of the United Nation's so-called Millennium Development Goals aims to improve the living conditions of at least 100 million slum-dwellers by 2020. The target is modest at best. An estimated 1 billion people currently live in slums, accounting for roughly a third of the world's urban population. And in some parts of the world, these impoverished districts have been growing very quickly. Between 1990 and 2007, the ranks of the world's slum-dwellers grew from 715 million to 998 million — a 40 percent increase. Asia's slum population is 581 million; sub-Saharan Africa, 199 million; and Latin America/Caribbean, 134 million.[7]

Despite the indisputable evidence of the spread of extreme urban poverty, these informal settlements represent a massive blind spot in official statistics. Many governments in the developing world don't accurately count slum populations in their censuses, fail to record whether slum residents own or rent their premises, and strongly resist demands to extend basic municipal services into sprawling shanty towns.

Slum Dwellers as a Percentage of Urban Population

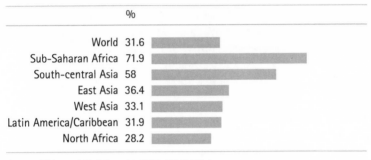

	%
World	31.6
Sub-Saharan Africa	71.9
South-central Asia	58
East Asia	36.4
West Asia	33.1
Latin America/Caribbean	31.9
North Africa	28.2

Source: Globe and Mail, June 21, 2007; UN Habitat

2006–2007, the poorest fifth of the world's population accounts for less than 1 percent of global consumption. Much of this poverty, however, is now urban, and increasingly concentrated in thousands of shanty towns. "Slums in many cities are no longer just marginalized neighborhoods housing a relatively small proportion of the urban population," the Habitat report observed. "[I]n many cities, they are the dominant type of human settlement, carving their way into the fabric of modern day cities…"[8]

The degree of urban poverty in the South varies significantly. In North African nations like Tunisia and Morocco, as well as many Latin American cities in Brazil and Mexico, slum population growth has been leveling off or falling due to progressive social policies and gradual increases in living standards. Today, the established favelas of cities like Rio de Janeiro — despite persistent drug-related crime and high levels of violence — have gradually moved beyond their shanty-town origins as residents establish thriving local businesses and social institutions, erect sturdier dwellings, and gain some access to municipal services and utilities. Still, the crowded favelas of São Paulo are home to 2.5 million people, about a tenth of the metropolitan population.[9] Likewise, Mexico City since the 1990s has been surrounded by a steadily growing ring of informal housing.

Urban poverty tends to be far more pronounced in South Asian countries like Bangladesh and Pakistan, and in much of sub-Saharan Africa, where the proportion of slum-dwellers doubled between 1990 and 2005. In some African cities, such as Addis Ababa and Nairobi, the majority of the residents live in slums. They contend with daily crises such as epidemic levels of HIV/AIDs and little by way of a formal economy.

The rapid urbanization taking place in some parts of the South — triggered by the mechanization of the agricultural sector — has not been accompanied by the provision of urban manufacturing jobs. "Since the mid-1980s," notes urban critic Mike Davis, "the great industrial cities of the South — Bombay, Johannesburg, Buenos Aires, Belo Horizonte, and São Paulo — have all suffered massive plant closures and tendential de-industrialization."[10] Consequently, in a city like São Paulo, favela-dwellers face tough economic choices: some must commute for up to eight hours each day to work as domestics in the city's wealthy neighborhoods, while many teens and young men opt instead to join gangs that oversee the flourishing drug trade.[11] In Indian cities like Calcutta, meanwhile, thousands of women and girls must work as prostitutes in crowded red-light districts where cramped homes double as brothels.

These extremes of urban poverty are strongly associated with precarious housing conditions (see What Is a Slum?) that serve to further disenfranchise slum residents. In shanty towns, dwellings often have mud floors and are made of nondurable materials such as scrap lumber, sheet metal and tarps. Shared or pirated electrical wires are strung up haphazardly between these makeshift homes. The result is that they are overcrowded, lack proper ventilation, and don't meet basic fire and building code standards.

Nor are they situated on land suitable for residential dwellings. Urban slums have traditionally sprung up on marginal or risky land — steep slopes, flood plains, swamps, contaminated sites adjacent to factories or transportation corridors, even on garbage dumps. Residential structures may be especially vulnerable to seismic activity, contamination or ocean storms.

Water and Sanitation

Lack of access to "improved drinking water" is a dominant daily hardship associated with living in dense, polluted shanty towns. An estimated 170 million people in urban areas do not have access to it. And because of rural-urban migration, this number is increasing. For example, in Nigeria in 1990, 80 percent of urban-dwellers had access to improved water, but by 2004, the total had dropped to only 67 percent.[12] By Western standards, the UN's definition of "improved drinking water" includes water from sources that generally don't pass muster in affluent northern cities — not just household connections, but shared public standpipes, pumps, wells, springs and rainwater.

Local and national governments in some parts of the developing world try to conceal their water access problems by inflating official statistics on the availability of clean water to urban dwellers, even in the poorest areas. The reality is that clean, affordable water — for drinking, bathing and washing — often remains unavailable to the residents of slums. Indeed, in countries where the urban water supply is scant or inconsistent, water-related illnesses — including malaria and diarrhea — account for a disproportionate share of hospital visits.

One direct consequence of the failure of municipal authorities to provide clean drinking water has been the emergence of what Mike Davis characterizes as an "extortionate" trade in water in the poorest areas. "Water sales is a lucrative industry in poor cities," he observes. "Nairobi…is an egregious example, where politically connected entrepreneurs resell municipal water (which costs very little to families wealthy enough to afford a tap) in the slums at exorbitant prices." He points out that in Luanda, the poorest households spend about one-seventh of their income on water "that private companies simply pump from the nearby, sewage-polluted Bengo River."[13]

In many shanty towns that lack a decent water supply, sanitation systems are also either rudimentary or, in many cases, nonexistent. Streets are divided by open sewers and raw waste is dumped into local bodies of water without being treated.

Some slums have partially functioning waste systems. In a Mumbai squatter community called Sanjay Gandhi Nagar, about 300 families share two toilet blocks with ten stalls in each, writes Robert Neuwirth in his account of life in shanty towns. "Many families," he says, "have built toilets right into their homes, but they don't use them because the community has no sewers, only small trenches covered with paving stones, and residents worry that the heavy usage will plug up the channels and flood the streets with waste."[14]

Yet in many other cities, the infrastructure simply doesn't exist. These conditions prevail in desperately poor megacities in Africa, like Kinshasa, but also in Asian metropolises like Jakarta and Manila, where, as Mike Davis points out, gleaming office towers sit in the middle of a huge urban region where as few as 10 percent of residents live in dwellings that are linked to sewer systems.[15]

Quite apart from the drastic environmental and health consequences, the lack of this most basic form of municipal infrastructure exacts a harsh psychological toll on those who live in these slums, particularly women. "The absence of decent toilets in impoverished neighborhoods violates residents' right to privacy and is an affront to their dignity," observes UN Habitat's 2007 report on the world's cities. "Being deprived of adequate sanitation facilities is the most direct and most dehumanizing — but least often acknowledged — consequence of poverty."[16]

Slum Clearance, Squatters and Tenure

In mid-2007, Indian state officials and a leading Mumbai architect launched an ambitious plan to redevelop Dharavi, a warren-like shanty town of 600,000 that occupies a square mile of prime turf on the peninsula near the city's financial core. Government officials issued an international request for proposals that would see the slum cleared and replaced by factories, offices, apartment blocks, condos and sports facilities. The $2.3 billion project includes a plan to rehouse 57,000 of the Dharavi slum-dwellers in free apartments.[17]

While the proponents of the Dharavi scheme claim that their approach could rid the developing world of urban slums, the proposal is merely one of the more recent attempts to demolish megacity shanty towns and evict the occupants, many of whom migrated from the poverty or violence of rural areas and lack any legal claim to their makeshift dwellings. UN Habitat statistics suggest that the pace of forcible evictions escalated during the 2000s, especially in sub-Saharan Africa and Asia.

In some cases, authorities justify slum clearance by stating that the land is needed for infrastructure, such as highways or dams; in other cases, the land has been designated for redevelopment or urban beautification. Either way, the result is an escalation of human misery, thanks to the destruction of communities with internal social structures and informal economies: "It is not uncommon for evicted families to sleep out in the open around the demolished site without food or basic amenities," says UN Habitat. "Children and women are particularly vulnerable in such situations. Incidents of rape and killing of victims during and after eviction exercises have been reported in many places."

State action against the urban poor isn't unique to the developing world. In wealthy cities, low-income individuals and families remain vulnerable to discrimination and harassment from landlords, forced evictions, and police operations to rid downtown areas of homeless individuals and squatter communities occupying fallow public or private property. Such campaigns underscore the persistent mismatch between the needs of an urban population and a city's social and physical infrastructure.

In the developing world, huge numbers of slum-dwellers have little or no legal claim to their homes, or even recourse to tenant protection laws. Many shanty towns spring up on unused government land, and the dwellings themselves may be rented out by property developers or obtained by bribing local officials. The occupants may lack the most basic evidence of tenure — utility bills, leases, deeds of ownership.

Various forms of de facto ownership have evolved in some countries after years of skirmishes between authorities, who bulldoze shanty towns, and squatters, who quickly rebuild them. About half the citizens of Istanbul live in semilegal *gecekondu* homes. Robert Neuwirth says that "For years, Turkey's squatters built at night to take advantage of an ancient legal precept that said, essentially, that if they started construction at dusk and were moved in by sunrise without being discovered by the authorities, they gained legal standing and could not be evicted without a court fight." He also tells of a squatter city of 300,000, called Sultanbeyli, where "nobody owns, but everybody builds."[18] Similarly, in Brazil's well-established favelas, occupants can obtain a deed recognizing their ownership of a building, albeit not the land beneath it.

Beyond such local solutions, the deeper question is whether there's a right to land and property. Some reformers believe that property ownership is an important tool for raising living standards in the slums, squatter communities and shanty towns of the developing world. Yet many developing nations lack the government institutions needed to document and police land ownership. And, as other observers point out, most cities in wealthier nations have large populations of tenants — households that may not own land but can count on the rule of law to protect them from arbitrary evictions. With the rapid growth of developing world shanty towns, there's clearly a pressing need for a parallel system of tenant laws and rights designed to protect the world's newest and poorest urbanites.

Poverty and Local Democracy

The squalid living conditions that exist in the world's megacities pose a monumental dilemma for local and national governments, international aid agencies, and, of course, the millions fated to live in slums. There's no consensus about how to solve the problems. Some advocate massive infusions of development aid and improved access to education, while others believe in market-based reforms such as trade liberalization and the provision of micro-loans to help megacity residents establish viable small businesses. In some areas, governments and business elites favor top-down solutions, such as large-scale urban redevelopment schemes, while grassroots slum-dweller groups believe they know best how to improve their communities.

Yet from the point of view of local government, the relentless expansion of megacity slums raises a profound question about the nature of urban citizenship in the twenty-first century. Economic migrants who have flocked to shanty towns become part of the broader metropolitan fabric, regardless of local officials' intentions. So when slum-dwellers are systematically deprived of basic municipal services and subjected to forced evictions, the message is clear: these people have no legitimate claim on the urban spaces where they live, while local governments have no responsibility to attend to the needs of these makeshift communities.

In 1989, antipoverty activists in the south Brazilian state capital of Porto Alegre persuaded municipal leaders to adopt a much more participatory form of local government. They created a system for developing spending priorities that is guided by community-level citizen assemblies. In the intervening years, the municipality has sharply stepped up its investment in improving basic sanitation and building new schools and housing complexes. The widely lauded result has been a wholesale shift in the city's political culture and measurable improvements in many indicators of urban well-being.[19]

Porto Alegre's model has been taken up in almost 200 cities across Brazil and other Latin American countries. Such reforms are a reminder that urban poverty is as much a political problem as anything else. Can the inhabitants of shanty towns and favelas make their voices heard? In dictatorships and failed states, the question is moot, of course. But megacity slums exist in many democratic or quasi-democratic nations, where the poor have come to outnumber the more affluent segments of urban society. As Neuwirth writes of Mumbai, "The squatters are the majority, so they are the city. When they fully understand that, politics and policies will change for the better."[20]

Chapter 7
Crime, Epidemics and Terrorism

"Over time," observes historian Joel Kotkin, "no urban system can survive persistent chaos."[1]

Concern about safety and well-being are not unique to city-dwellers, but the crowded nature of urban living can produce distinct conditions that leave residents feeling fearful or insecure about violent crime, war, terrorist attacks or the threat of contagious disease. No city can ever provide a sense of iron-clad security for all its residents, all the time. But when anxiety about urban danger reaches a saturation point, the social fabric of cities begins to fray. Those with means flee or isolate themselves behind walls and security systems. Infected groups become pariahs. Businesses relocate to safer areas, and commerce declines. Suspicion of strangers, the poor and immigrants rises, weakening the social ties that make populous urban communities livable. The collective energy of the city shifts from more high-minded pursuits — cultural activity, scientific inquiry, commercial innovation — to defensive strategies, such as increased policing.

There are, of course, many factors that accelerate the erosion of urban safety. Some have to do with the fact that large cities are concentrated population centers, where millions of people are potentially exposed to various sources of external danger, such as invasions, suicide bombers or epidemics. Sectarian violence among rival religious or ethnic groups can transform cities into war zones, as has happened in Belfast, Beirut and Sarajevo. At the same time, cities themselves may create the conditions that lead to an increase in crime — for example, isolating the very poor or racial minorities in low-income ghettos with few jobs. Lastly, urban chaos can be the direct consequence of national or international policies, such as weak gun laws, underfunded public health programs and militaristic campaigns intended to curb drug use.

As the world's population becomes increasingly urbanized and mobile, the problem of how to build and sustain safe cities takes on greater importance. In the post-9/11 era, urban security is closely related to geopolitics. But there's much more to building safe cities than tough-minded policing and security. Safe and healthy cities are also inclusive, forward-looking places whose residents understand that urban well-being is as much about preventing crime, poverty and disease as it is about struggling to control the chaos after the fact.

Urban Crime

In the 1970s, the leading daily newspapers in Detroit and Chicago became embroiled in a grim form of rivalry: on page one, each published an ongoing year-to-date tally of murders as the two cities competed to become the homicide capital of the US. But in the 1990s, violent crime in many large American cities abruptly began to fall, sometimes quite dramatically, in the case of New York City.

The Big Apple's crime trend was part of an international phenomenon: surveys of thirty-three cities with more than 100,000 residents conducted in the 1990s showed an overall drop in victimization, both for property crimes and assaults. Despite the stabilization of crime rates worldwide, UN Habitat notes that almost three in four city-dwellers in Latin America and Africa were victims of crime between 2001 and 2006.[2]

There are many explanations for the improvements in crime rates in some urban areas. Some analysts argued that the changes reflected overall improvements in the economy or demographic shifts (i.e., crime rates are higher when there are more young men in a given population). But one of the most popular explanations revolved around the "broken windows" theory, developed by professors James Q. Wilson and George Kelling. They argued that when cities tolerate the accumulation of minor property crime, such as broken windows and graffiti on abandoned buildings, urban spaces come to feel less safe. Law-abiding citizens withdraw or move elsewhere, and these increasingly derelict areas come to be dominated by gangs and the homeless.

Journalist Malcolm Gladwell, author of "The Tipping Point," points out that in New York City in the 1990s, the police and other city agencies, at the urging of Mayor Rudolph Giuliani, decided to put the broken windows theory into practice. They launched aggressive campaigns to eradicate graffiti, chase away loiterers, shut down drug dens and force the homeless off the streets. The overall effect, argues Gladwell, is that residents regained a sense of safety and this attitudinal shift spread like an epidemic.[3] New Yorkers took back the city and made it less inviting to criminals or gangs, thereby precipitating a drop in violent crime. As of 2007, NYC's murder rate was 75 percent lower than it was in 1993; the city experienced a similar drop in all crime categories.

Urban Crime: Personal Perception and Statistical Reality

Among criminologists, it's a well-known phenomenon: the public's perception of crime may have little to do with actual crime trends. And though well understood, these discrepancies can have a powerful impact on how cities manage their law enforcement agencies, how families make decisions about where to live, and where businesses choose to locate. In Australia, for example, social attitudes surveys conducted in 2003 found that the majority of respondents felt crime had increased a little or a lot over the previous two years. Older people in particular felt crime was becoming increasingly serious. Yet the Australian Institute of Criminology observed that "according to the International Crime Victimisation Survey, crime victimisation rates in Australia declined between 2000 and 2004, from 24 percent to 17 percent."[4]

There are various explanations for this discrepancy. Sensational media coverage of violent crime fuels the fear of crime and may contribute to the creation of entrenched public attitudes about the pervasiveness of lawless behavior. Those stereotypes are then reinforced and exaggerated by the entertainment industry.

But there are other factors that can be attributed to the prevailing political culture of a given city. One is the degree of separation between affluent urbanites and disenfranchised groups, such as visible minorities and the poor. Urban segregation stokes the "otherness" of those who venture outside their designated enclaves. Another factor relates to the use of public spaces. Well-used streets and parks may be perceived to be safer than they actually are, simply because they're busy.

Lastly, the media may unwittingly stigmatize or label certain neighborhoods or intersections as dangerous by virtue of the coverage of violent crimes that occur in those areas. These labels, and the inferred reputations they carry, can persist for years and decades, despite the fact that the residents of those areas know the ground-level reality to be quite different from the stereotype. The result is that names like "East LA," "South Bronx" or "Jane-Finch" (in Toronto) not only become equated with violent crime, so do the law-abiding residents of those areas.

It's true that when streets *feel* safe, they may actually become safer. Jane Jacobs coined the phrase "eyes on the street" to describe blocks lined with homes or apartments where front windows and porches give residents a clear view of what is happening in the public spaces in front of their homes. Busy sidewalks, well-lit parks and highly visible schoolyards, in turn, tend to be safer than areas that seem abandoned and lonely. Indeed, these details are now accepted principles of urban design.

Indeed, we would be naïve to conclude that tough-on-crime and anti-gang policing are sufficient to combat urban violence. Preventive measures are equally important. In low-income neighborhoods with high unemployment, municipalities and other local agencies must ensure that schools, community centers, libraries and recreation facilities are adequately funded so young people have alternatives to crime.

Restrictions on access to lethal weapons are another key factor in containing urban crime. In the US, where firearms are readily accessible and gun-control laws tend to be weak, gun-related crime rates remain substantially higher than those in comparably sized cities in other countries in the developed world. According to Statistics Canada, "Canada's 2006 firearm homicide rate was nearly six times lower than the United States. But it was about three times higher than the rate in Australia and six times higher than in England and Wales."[5]

Finally, there is a strong relationship between the degree of income disparity and urban crime rates. British sociologist Richard Wilkinson, author of *Unhealthy Societies: The Afflictions of Inequality*, says nations that are able to reduce the economic distance between the most and least affluent groups tend to be healthier, with a higher overall quality of life. By contrast, some of the world's most economically or socially segregated cities, like Johannesburg, South Africa, are also the most dangerous and unstable. In São Paulo, a city of 23 million, there's both great wealth and desperate poverty, and increasingly, bitter feuds between a brutal police force and the gangs that control the city's favelas and prisons. The running battles erupted into a mass inmate rebellion and orchestrated attacks on police and city property in May 2006.

As journalist William Langewiesche noted, São Paulo, in its transformation into a global business capital, had become "an archipelago of innumerable little fortresses where a large population of the fortunate lived and worked in near-total isolation from the poor." The social disintegration and associated increase in criminal activity is due to entrenched poverty, which the government hasn't been able to confront. Instead, Langewiesche reports, São Paulo police authorities opted for a crackdown, which in turn spurred a violent insurrection by the ruthless gangs that control vast empires from Brazil's overcrowded prisons.[6]

Drugs and Urban Crime

Laws prohibiting the sale and possession of narcotics have undoubtedly fueled urban crime and the proliferation of guns across much of the world. While legal bans on opium date back to the nineteenth century, concerted international efforts to contain the global drug trade began in earnest in the early 1970s, when American president Richard Nixon launched the first "war on drugs."

By then, however, there was clear evidence of the link between illicit substances and urban crime. During the 1920s and 1930s, temperance groups in North America persuaded lawmakers to make the production, sale and distribution of alcohol illegal, with the result that the entire industry went underground.

When a widely used commodity like alcohol is criminalized, the individuals and organizations that make and sell it don't disappear, but they can no longer count on the protection of the law to safeguard their investments. Normal businesses can call the police if they've been robbed, or resort to the courts to deal with suppliers or customers that don't pay. No such protections exist when a substance is deemed illegal, even though consumer demand persists and may even grow as a result of the ban. Producers and distributors — outlaws functioning in a legal gray zone — must resort to self-defense to protect their inventories and supply chain.

After the US Congress repealed the prohibition laws, the liquor smuggling trade quickly transformed into a large and legal enterprise that didn't need to protect itself with guns and intimidation. It began to pay taxes as well. The lifting of such legal sanctions also gradually opened up the opportunity for the public, government and the liquor industry itself to consider serious substance abuse issues, such as drunk driving and alcoholism. The gambling industry has experienced a very similar transformation.

In the case of illicit drugs, the cure has been worse than the disease. While drugs like heroin, cocaine and marijuana were originally banned because they were seen to cause antisocial and at times dangerous behavior, the enormous amount of violence unleashed by the drug prohibition has likely caused at least as much harm. In smuggling gateway cities such as Los Angeles or Miami, gangs battle one another for control of the drug trade. Meanwhile, in producer nations, like Colombia, cities like Medellín have been consumed by intense violence among heavily armed drug cartels.

In recent years, the Internet has cut into the traditional drug distribution trade, as information on easily fabricated synthetic drugs, such as crystal meth, has become widely available. What's more, part of the production end of the drug trade has shifted out of remote rural areas in South America and into drug factories that operate inconspicuously from suburban homes fitted out with labs and hydroponics equipment. In Canadian cities such as Vancouver and Toronto, where marijuana use is very high,[7] hundreds of grow-ops have popped up in neighborhoods. These homes are noteworthy because the windows are often lined with foil, while visitors come and go at odd hours. But although recreational marijuana use is widespread and relatively benign, the grow-ops themselves pose a risk — they tend to be poorly ventilated firetraps, and the dealers who operate them are often armed.

Countries with liberal drug laws, like the Netherlands, attempted to counter the criminality associated with drug trafficking by legalizing marijuana. Major cities such as Amsterdam licensed cafes where customers could purchase and smoke pot or hashish. Some other countries have attempted to follow suit, despite pressure from the US.

In the late 1980s, the notion of a safe zone for drug use evolved to include heroin consumption by the addicts who had congregated in European cities like Zurich. Despite antidrug laws and aggressive enforcement, many European cities couldn't control the trade in highly addictive injection drugs, and the users, in turn, were responsible for a proliferation of nuisance crimes — such as prostitution and break-and-enter — to finance their habits. They were also becoming a public health risk due to the spread of HIV/AIDs among intravenous drug users, sex-trade workers and their customers.

Rather than pursuing futile attempts to prosecute drug addicts, authorities in cities like Frankfurt, Germany, established so-called safe injection sites with the goal of treating the problem as a public health issue. Registered addicts bring their drugs to these facilities, receive clean needles and shoot up in supervised, hygienic conditions. The centers are also staffed with medical personnel, social workers and representatives of affordable housing agencies, all of whom can try to guide addicts toward detox programs, healthcare providers and other forms of support.

In 2002, Vancouver established North America's first safe injection facility in the city's Downtown Eastside, a desperately poor area near the city's port that had become a hub of drug dealing and prostitution. The move came amid intense controversy and outraged US drug enforcement officials. But its supporters persuaded government officials that it no longer made any sense to cycle homeless addicts through a criminal justice system ill-equipped to address the illness of drug addiction. Rather, police and government officials pursue "harm reduction" measures — such as needle exchanges and more responsive treatment programs — to contain the health risks.

European studies show a reduction in minor drug-related street crime, as well as a sharp drop in the number of overdose deaths, in cities with safe injection sites, because addicts are able to shoot up in places where medical personnel are able to respond quickly to emergencies. What's more, in Vancouver, researchers have found that the presence of the safe injection facility has led to a reduction in risky behavior, such as needle sharing, and an increase in the number of addicts referred to counseling and mental health services.⁸ Still, addicts continue to gravitate to Vancouver's Downtown Eastside, and the petty crime associated with the illegal drug trade persists.

Epidemics and Cities

The story of Vancouver's safe injection site offers a reminder that the need to protect public health is a core urban responsibility, and one that is intimately connected to the broader population's sense of security and well-being. As we saw in previous chapters, epidemics decimated many cities in the Middle Ages as highly infectious diseases felled millions of residents living in crowded and unhygienic conditions.

When smallpox swept through Montreal in the late nineteenth century, the ensuing public panic revealed, among other things, that no one really knew who should be assuming responsibility for containing the disease. Local officials, it's true, had the power to quarantine the sick, but they were hampered in their ability to compel residents to be vaccinated against the disease. The epidemic, moreover, was linked to inadequate sanitation and water systems in the small surrounding municipalities. As the city's first medical officer of health said at the time, the provincial and federal governments needed to involve themselves in such situations by collecting health statistics and forcing municipalities to establish boards of health.⁹

During the twentieth century, dramatic advances in epidemiology, sanitation and public health practice led to the eradication of many lethal diseases (see The Spanish Flu Pandemic). Vaccinations once considered controversial are now commonplace. And in many cities, public health departments have turned their attention to other population

The Spanish Flu Pandemic of 1918–19

In the waning months of World War I, a particularly lethal strain of influenza began to crop up in different parts of the world, and quickly ignited a global pandemic that killed between 20 million and 40 million people. It is considered to be the worst epidemic in human history. The disease spread among soldiers fighting in the war and then traveling home once it ended. That strain of flu proved to be especially deadly for young adults, and sufferers could succumb within hours or days of contracting the disease.

As public health officials scrambled to contain the outbreak, they began to focus their efforts on ventilation as well as quarantining victims. Because the influenza microbe spread on tiny droplets coughed out or exhaled by those who had been infected, the disease thrived in crowded conditions, such as troop carriers and rooming houses. In many cities in Europe and North America, public health agencies ordered the closure of places where crowds congregated – theaters, dance halls, even funerals. People were encouraged to walk to work instead of taking streetcars, and businesses were asked to stagger opening hours to mitigate crowding. There was considerable controversy on both sides of the Atlantic about whether or not to close elementary schools. Some cities distributed gauze masks, to be worn in public.

The legacy of the 1918–19 flu epidemic can still be seen today: hospital wards are less crowded and beds are separated by dividers. Personal hygiene techniques, such as thorough hand-washing, are commonly used. And in recent years, flu vaccines have come to be part of the arsenal used by public health practitioners to prevent the outbreak of future flu epidemics.[10]

afflictions, such as air quality, hepatitis C, childhood diabetes, HIV/AIDS, second-hand smoke and tuberculosis among the homeless.

Yet in 2002 and 2003, a sudden outbreak of a pneumonia-like disease known as sudden acute respiratory syndrome (SARS) — which spread rapidly from China's Guangdong province to cities such as Hong Kong, Singapore and Toronto — vividly illustrated the new global trajectories of infectious diseases, as well as differing levels of urban preparedness. Researchers have warned for years of the looming risk of mass epidemics related to new drug-resistant strains of bacteria or avian flu. But for urbanities accustomed to the relatively hygienic conditions of affluent twentieth-century cities, the SARS epidemic represented their first encounter with the onset of a poorly understood and frequently lethal disease.

The impact SARS had on Toronto in the spring of 2003 offers a preview of how future epidemics will affect large cities. The original case involved an elderly woman who'd been infected in China and flew to Toronto without knowing she was ill. As the disease spread among hospital patients and health care workers who had inadvertently been exposed to the earliest cases, panic began to take hold. Hundreds of people were quarantined. Consumers stopped patronizing Asian restaurants. Convention and tour groups abruptly canceled events scheduled for later that summer after the World Health Organization issued a travel advisory. Hospitals and public health agencies were caught unprepared, while health care workers faced extraordinarily frightening and stressful conditions as they risked catching the disease on the job precisely when their services were most needed. The epidemic ran through two waves, and it finally abated in June, almost four months after the first patient was diagnosed.

A government review of the SARS crisis described the epidemic as "the perfect storm" because it was an unknown disease that struck a city ill-prepared to fight such outbreaks. The review criticized funding cutbacks that had left hospitals and public health agencies without the resources needed to prepare for such events. In Vancouver, by contrast, provincial labor officials had trained health care workers in the proper use of special masks and other safety systems designed to protect them from catching contagious diseases while administering emergency procedures to ill patients.

While the SARS epidemic had a jarring impact on the afflicted cities, it can't begin to compare to the magnitude of the HIV/AIDS pandemic that has ravaged so much of sub-Saharan Africa, particularly the poor who live in urban regions. "Trends indicate that the disease first appears in cities and then diffuses to rural areas along major road networks," according to UN Habitat. Truck drivers, travelers and sex workers have been implicated in spreading the disease. HIV/AIDS is significantly more prevalent in urban areas than in rural regions in countries like Lesotho, Kenya and Zambia. These infection patterns aren't limited to Africa: in Latin American countries like Argentina, HIV is concentrated in the largest cities, and an estimated 65 per cent of HIV infections occur in the capital, Buenos Aires.[11]

When the AIDS crisis first struck US cities such as New York and San Francisco, the disease was most prevalent among gay men, intravenous drug users and hemophiliacs who had received tainted blood transfusions. Activists pressured governments to fund research and prevention/information programs. By the latter 1990s, these efforts began to bear fruit, with the result that HIV infection today is no longer a guaranteed death sentence. Costly drug therapies and other treatment approaches have transformed AIDS into something more like a serious but chronic condition.

The face of HIV/AIDS in the cities of the developing world is very different. "High risk sexual behavior, fractured family networks and poor access to health services appear to account for the high prevalence of HIV/AIDS in Africa's urban centers," according to UN Habitat, which notes that the proportion of the urban poor with multiple sexual partners is significantly higher than that of the rural poor. In countries like India, meanwhile, a large proportion of sex workers don't require their customers to use condoms. And in urban slums throughout the developing world, children and teens begin experimenting with sexual activity at a younger age than the residents of wealthier areas.[12]

The magnitude of Africa's AIDS crisis is overwhelming and extends well beyond the urban sphere. There are millions of orphans and families unable to earn a living due to the death of a breadwinner. Economically, the AIDS pandemic has contributed to the steep decline of some African countries, which have watched their labor forces shrink.

High pharmaceutical costs and tattered health systems have prevented the widespread use of the drug therapies used to fight AIDS in the developed world. Nor has it helped that some African heads of state reject conventional treatment methods and the use of condoms. The Bush administration exacerbated the problem by making foreign aid funding for condom programs conditional on recipient countries agreeing to promote abstinence and condemn prostitution.[13]

The consequences of the AIDS pandemic, however, will be felt increasingly acutely in cities, for the simple reason that so much of the developing world is in the throes of rapid urbanization.

War, Political Violence and Cities
The history of warfare and conquest is riddled with accounts of the sacking of towns and cities that happened to be situated

in the path of an invading army or that occupied a strategically important location. During World War II, modern weaponry — long-range missiles, high-altitude bombers and then atomic bombs — ushered in a new era of urban destruction. Dresden, Berlin, London and Stalingrad (now Volgograd) sustained extensive wartime damage and mass casualties, while the nuclear warheads dropped on Hiroshima and Nagasaki leveled both cities and killed hundreds of thousands of civilians. In 1944, on the eve of the Allies' liberation of Paris, Hitler famously ordered his troops to set fire to the city, but his generals refused to follow orders.

In the postwar era, however, large cities have increasingly become the stage for organized political terrorism. This new reality didn't start on September 11, 2001. During the 1980s and 1990s, the provisional Irish Republican Army detonated bombs (or issued bomb threats) in London and Manchester to pressure the British government to withdraw troops from Northern Ireland. Suicide bombers have set off dozens of bombs in Israeli cities, killing hundreds of civilians. But it took al Qaeda's unprecedented attack on New York's World Trade Center to drive home the message that busy and economically robust cities are appealing targets for terrorist organizations.

This lesson has been borne out repeatedly in cities like Madrid, London, Jerusalem and Baghdad — all places where radicals and insurgent groups have strategically targeted crowded urban spaces. But when terrorists mount surprise attacks in subways, office towers, outdoor markets and restaurants, they are not only aiming to kill innocent civilians. Such attacks can rapidly disable the commercial and transportation infrastructures of large cities; the crippling effects may be felt long after the carnage initially occurs.

Berlin and the Urban Legacy of the Cold War

At the end of World War II, the Allies carved up Berlin into four quadrants. The political seat of Prussia and later Germany for centuries, Berlin was Hitler's capital; indeed, the Nazi dictator had ordered his chief architect, Albert Speer, to develop plans to transform Berlin into the hub of an empire on the scale of Ancient Rome. By 1945, however, parts of Berlin had been extensively destroyed during the final siege of the city.

Though Berlin sat in the middle of East Germany, it remained a partially open city until 1961, when the Soviet Union and the East German government hastily erected a wall — actually a pair of high concrete walls astride a strip of mined no-man's-land — along the border between the USSR's quadrant and the areas controlled by the US, France and Britain. The German authorities demolished buildings in the no-man's-land, including large swaths of what had been the city's commercial core.

While the Berlin Wall became the defining symbol of the Cold War, it had a profound effect on the way the city functioned. The wall divided families and neighborhoods. Berlin's subway system meandered on either side of the wall, but the stations on the east side were closed. Meanwhile, a broad strip of land on the west side of the wall fell into disuse during the Cold War. It turned into a sullen, largely abandoned area bounded by the graffiti-covered wall and visited mainly by tourists who would climb up viewing platforms to peer across the no-man's-land.

The fall of the Berlin Wall in November 1989 set the stage for the collapse of the Soviet Empire and the re-unification of Germany in 1991. Berlin once again became the capital, and the city embarked on a rapid campaign to redevelop the extensive amount of fallow space where the wall had stood. Beginning in 1995, that strip of central Berlin was completely rebuilt by the world's most prominent architects. The revitalization allowed historic streets, like Potsdamer Platz, to be restored to prominence. As for the Berlin Wall itself, apart from a few segments maintained as a historic monument, all evidence of its divisive presence has been erased from Berlin's cityscape.

In the wake of 9/11, many municipal, regional and national governments began to rethink the challenge of ensuring urban safety in the age of terrorism. Some local governments have reluctantly followed London's lead, installing extensive networks of closed-circuit television cameras that are trained on public spaces.[14] Municipal agencies are changing the way they design and deploy garbage bins, which have been used to conceal crude bombs. Subways, water treatment facilities, power plants, government buildings, major tourist attractions and other important urban assets are now much more closely policed than before 9/11. Yet the reality is that bustling urban cores can never be managed like the controlled access areas of airports. If a terrorist group succeeds in eluding national or international intelligence agencies, cities offer countless venues where such organizations can perpetrate political violence.

Interestingly, some cities that have experienced sustained political violence or terrorist attacks — London, Beirut, Jerusalem — display remarkable fortitude in the face of political violence. Indeed, other forces — sprawl, racial conflict and economic decline — exact as much, or even more, damage to the continuing health of cities, as has been the case in once-thriving industrial hubs like Detroit and Glasgow.

The residents of cities caught up in the midst of such strife have little choice but to find ways of adapting to terrifying conditions. For example, between the early 1970s and the late 1990s, local officials in Belfast were scrupulous about not inflaming the Protestant-Catholic tensions. The approach was to ensure that planning decisions were ethnically neutral while respecting the territorial divisions that had turned Northern Ireland's violence-ridden capital into a patchwork of walled neighborhoods.[15]

But for cities that have been divided or ripped apart by powerful geopolitical forces or national antagonisms, the problem of maintaining security invariably raises a deeper issue: how to bring about reconciliation at the level of urban neighborhoods? It's a question that confronts cities like Paris and London, where some disenfranchised or marginalized migrant workers living in low-income suburbs have been implicated in acts of political terrorism and rioting.

This difficult riddle has also confronted Johannesburg in the post-apartheid era. The city emerged from official segregation bearing the scars of stark racial splits: wealthy white enclaves and commercial areas in a metropolitan core surrounded by impoverished black townships (Alexandra and Soweto) situated about 16 kilometers (10 miles) from the city.

In 1991, after the end of apartheid, Johannesburg embarked on a difficult restructuring of its local and regional governments. The city at the time had a population of 2 million: 60 percent were black, 31 percent white. Four years later, Johannesburg's newly enfranchised black residents elected black majorities to the five municipal councils that oversee the region.

That democratic change in civic governance in South Africa's largest metropolis illustrates a basic question posed in Chapter 1: What is the nature, meaning and extent of urban citizenship in this urban century? It's not a theoretical problem. By extending urban citizenship to those who've been excluded, the city itself will invariably evolve. Today, the citizens of Johannesburg are being called upon to find collective solutions to the divisions and the difficulties that afflict their home.

While the task of bringing democracy and equality to

South Africa is obviously more than a municipal issue, the Johannesburg officials in charge of a newly constituted city government understood that they had to change the physical structure of the city in order to create conditions that would allow blacks to participate fully in urban life. The goal was to fill in the gaps between the black townships and the city's core with high-density development as a means of physically, and then socially, reconnecting Johannesburg's two solitudes. Urban leaders also sought to upgrade the physical and social infrastructure of the townships, although critics warned that investing public funds in these areas could unintentionally reinforce existing racial divisions.[16]

Did those changes produce a healthier city? In the years following the dismantling of apartheid, the city ceased to be off-limits to blacks and Indians. Thousands flocked into the core, while the white middle class fled. The result was a downtown increasingly neglected by municipal authorities. With one of the worst big city crime rates in the world, Johannesburg came to be dominated by abandoned buildings filled with squatters, many of whom were poor migrants from other countries in southern Africa. One high rise in particular came to symbolize the transformation: the cylindrical fifty-four-storey luxury apartment building known as Ponte City. "Within a year or two [of the end of apartheid]," reports the award-winning Canadian journalist Stephanie Nolen, "its 11 storeys of parking garage were being used as a dimly-lit brothel, drug lords operated brazenly out of the lobby and three stories of trash built up in the hollow core of the building. [The] Ponte went from byword of style to epicenter of crime and urban decay."[17]

More recently, Nolen reports, there's been evidence of rejuvenation in Johannesburg. A redevelopment agency has been working to restore the downtown, bring back businesses and lure the middle class out of the fortified compounds in the suburbs. Ponte City, in fact, was acquired by developers — one a white South African émigré; the other, the son of Moroccan immigrants who'd settled in Rotterdam. They have invested $14 million in restoring the iconic Johannesburg tower to its former luxury status. The developers vowed to find alternative downtown accommodation for the low-income tenants who had taken up residence in Ponte City's cheap apartments. As a Johannesburg development expert put it, "The impetus is there, the political attraction is there, a lot of things [are] going in its favor, but there are a lot of areas that need TLC before you can say we're on the road again."[18]

While changes in South Africa relate to a very specific political transformation, big cities everywhere are grappling with similar problems thanks to mass immigration, rapid urbanization, economic globalization and the widening gap between rich and poor. These powerful forces express themselves at the level of urban life, creating cityscapes that situate enclaves of entitlement next to zones of despair. The twenty-first-century metropolis will be a concentrated place of nearly unfathomable diversity — ethnic, social, economic, environmental, religious. Large cities have become a microcosm of everything that's taking place in this complex world. For good or ill, they are our future.

Cities Timeline

9000 BC Emergence of the earliest clan-based villages in the Nile River valley and Mesopotamia.

7500 to 6000 BC Jericho settled, construction of city walls.

3000 BC Evolution of the multifunction village as settlements include inhabitants with specialized skills, as well as priests, soldiers and rulers, and buildings with nondomestic functions, such as shrines, warehouses and citadels.

1000 BC Biblical legend has it that David, king of the Jews, establishes Jerusalem as his political capital.

753 BC Rome founded.

500–400 BC Golden era of Athens and the Greek *polis* or city-state.

331 BC Alexander the Great founds Alexandria, on the Nile Delta, and the city remains the capital of Egypt for nearly 1000 years.

50 BC to AD 100 Age of the Roman Empire. Rome and Luoyang (Honan), China, are the world's most populous cities.

AD 43 Romans found Londonium as an outpost colony.

330 Constantinople, later Istanbul, established as the new capital of the Roman Empire; it becomes the hub of Byzantium and later the seat of Ottoman rule.

969 Islamic Cairo founded.

1000 Cordova, Spain, and Kaifeng, China, are the world's two most populous cities.

1100s Venice becomes a major merchant power and an independent city.

1200s Toledo, Spain, becomes known as a cultural and academic center famous for the peaceful co-existence of Christians, Jews and Muslims. The latter two groups were expelled during the Crusades at the end of the 15th century.

1325 Aztecs establish Tenochtitlán as an imperial capital; it is subsequently destroyed and rebuilt by Spanish conquistadors as Mexico City.

1400s Artists, scientists and aristocratic patrons trigger the Renaissance in Florence.

1400s Timbuktu, in present-day Mali, emerges as a center for Islamic scholarship and culture.

1500 Beijing and Vijayanagar (south India) are the world's two most populous cities.

1603 Tokugawa shogunate takes power in Edo, later Tokyo, marking the beginning of a 250-year reign during which the city grew into one of the world's largest urban centers.

1624 Dutch traders establish the first permanent settlement on Manhattan, an island long inhabited by the Lenape First Nation and other native tribes.

Amsterdam, during this period, has become a powerful commercial hub, with trading ties throughout the New World and Asia.

1759 Battle of the Plains of Abraham, just outside Quebec City, sees British forces defeat the French and consolidate control over North American colonies.

1773 New England colonialists rebel against Britain during the Boston Tea Party, an antitax uprising that leads to the American Revolution three years later.

1750s to1830s Manchester develops into the world's first industrial city.

1800 Beijing and London are the world's two most populous cities.

1869 Opening of the Suez Canal, in Egypt, transforms Bombay (now Mumbai) into a major Eastern gateway for goods headed toward Western ports of call.

1871 Great Fire of Chicago, triggered when a cow knocks over a gas lantern; this event sets the stage for the redevelopment of the city according to the historic plan of Daniel Burnham.

1870s to 1914 Emergence of modern art and literary movements in Paris.

1890s Invention of the modern skyscraper using steel frame construction rather than masonry.

1900 London and New York are the world's two most populous cities.

1940 Bombing of London by Nazi air force during the Battle of Britain.

1945 to 1973 Postwar affluence, the baby boom and the mass production of the automobile in North America usher in the bedroom suburb.

1950 New York and London are the world's two most populous cities.

1960s Activist Jane Jacobs leads successful fight to block freeways into Lower

A Brief History of Sewers

The history of the sewer closely follows the evolution of cities, for the simple reason that no human settlement can exist without an effective way of disposing of waste. Here are some highlights, courtesy of sewerhistory.org, a not-for-profit website maintained by Jon Schladweiler, the historian of the Arizona Water and Pollution Control Association.

Babylon (Iraq), 4000 BC – streets paved with brick sewers and some homes built over cesspools; earliest clay drainage pipes.

Indus Civilization (Pakistan), 3000–2000 BC – houses with adjacent latrines and bathrooms, suggesting awareness of hygiene; some bathrooms connected to street sewers; manhole covers have been found.

Rome, 800 BC–AD 300 – public baths and latrines; waste thrown into gutters, but water

Manhattan, setting the stage for later victories by inner-city activists in San Francisco, Toronto and Vancouver.

1964 Japan introduces high-speed bullet trains between urban centers.

1973 Completion of the Sydney Opera House, one of the world's most iconic cultural structures.

April 1975 Pol Pot and the Khmer Rouge occupy Cambodian capital of Phnom Penh and begin the brutal mass evacuation of city-dwellers into the countryside, leading to the deaths of hundreds of thousands.

November 9, 1989 Fall of the Berlin Wall.

1990 China announces development of Pudong City, in Shanghai. Pudong has become the financial capital of China, home to hundreds of skyscrapers and relentless redevelopment.

1997 The ninety-nine-year British lease of Hong Kong expires and the city reverts to Chinese political rule.

September, 11, 2001 Terrorist attacks on New York City and Washington lead to the American invasion of Iraq and occupation of Baghdad.

2003 Tokyo, Japan, and Seoul, South Korea, are the world's most populous metropolitan regions.

2006 Greater Toronto emerges as the world's most multi-ethnic metropolis, with 45.7 percent of its residents born outside Canada.

2008 For the first time in human history, more people live in urban areas — in cities — than in the countryside.

---

from aqueducts routinely used to wash streets; introduction of lead pipes; completed in 510 BC, the city's main sewer remains in service today.

Europe, Dark and Middle Ages – decline of sanitation associated with rise of epidemics; streets were essentially open sewers, as residents threw their waste, collected in chamber pots, out of upper-storey windows; use of cesspits beneath buildings resulted in foul odors and soil saturated with human waste.

Paris, nineteenth century – construction of a modern sewer system, which eventually boasted a line for every street, totaling over 500 kilometers (311 miles).

US, nineteenth century – introduction of odorless pumping services to remove waste from residential cesspools; development of new technologies and materials to improve sewer pipe design; sewage pumping and flushing systems.

Notes

Chapter 1 **The Urban Century**

1. United Nations Population Fund, www.unfpa.org/swp/2007/english/ introduction.html.
2. Joel Kotkin, *The City: A Global History* (New York: Random House, 2005).
3. Takashi Machimura, "The Urban Restructuring Process in Tokyo in the 1980s: Transforming Tokyo into a World City," in *The Global Cities Reader*, Neil Brenner and Roger Keil, eds. (New York: Routledge, 2006), 145–53.
4. Aristotle, *The Politics*. Translated by Carnes Lord. (Chicago: University of Chicago Press, 1984), 37.
5. Ruth Eaton, *Ideal Cities* (London: Thames and Hudson, 2002).

Chapter 2 **Urban Forms and Functions**

1. Spiro Kostof, *The City Shaped: Urban Patterns and Meanings Through History* (London: Thames and Hudson, 1991), 29–30.
2. Ibid., 52.
3. Ibid., 48–49.
4. Lewis Mumford, *The City in History: Its Origins, Its Transformations, and Its Prospects* (New York: Harcourt, 1961), 96.
5. Kostof, *The City Shaped*, 37–40.
6. Anthony Tung, *Preserving the World's Great Cities: The Destruction and Renewal of the Historic Metropolis* (New York: Three Rivers Press, 2001), 160–67.
7. Kotkin, *The City*, 126.
8. Tung, *Preserving the World's Great Cities*, 407–408.
9. Ibid., 254.
10. Kotkin, *The City*, xxi.
11. Peter Hall, *Cities in Civilization* (New York: Random House, 1998), 44.
12. Kotkin, *The City*, 27.
13. Tung, *Preserving the World's Great Cities*, 34.
14. Kostof, *The City Shaped*, 19.
15. Tung, *Preserving the World's Great Cities*, 145.
16. Kotkin, *The City*, 31–32.
17. Ibid., 78.
18. Ibid., 79.
19. Ibid., 67.
20. Ibid., 87.

21. Sources: Canadian 2006 Census: www12.statcan.ca/english/census06/ analysis/immcit/city_life.cfm; http://news.bbc.co.uk/2/shared/spl/hi/uk/05/ born_abroad/around_britain/html/london.stm.

22. Tung, *Preserving the World's Great Cities*, 107.

23. Richard Grant and Jan Nijman, "Globalization and the Corporate Geography of Cities in the Less-developed World," in *The Global Cities Reader*, 229–35.

24. Saskia Sassen, "Cities in a World Economy" (1994) in *The Global Cities Reader*, 70–74.

25. Riccardo Petrella, quoted in "World-city Network: A New Metageography?" in *The Global Cities Reader*, 102.

26. Sassen, "Cities and Communities," *The Global Cities Reader*, 87.

Chapter 3 **Sprawl Happens**

1. In the US, the growth of the suburbs wasn't merely an economic phenomenon. It was subsidized by the state through policies such as the federal government's highway building campaigns, low-interest mortgages for returning soldiers, and a provision in the tax code allowing homeowners to deduct mortgage payments from their income taxes.

2. Sara Clemence, "Most Expensive Gated Communities in America 2004," *Forbes Magazine*, www.forbes.com/realestate/2004/11/19/cx_sc_ 1119home.html.

3. University of Bristol, School of Policy Studies, www.bristol.ac.uk/sps/ cnrpapersword/cnr12sum.doc.

4. Mike Davis, *Planet of Slums* (New York: Verso, 2006), 116–20.

5. Jane Jacobs, *The Death and Life of Great American Cities* (New York: Alfred A. Knopf, 1961), 205–206.

6. Kotkin, *The City*, 124.

7. www.citymayors.com/statistics/largest-cities-density-125.html.

8. Joel Garreau, *Edge City: Life on the New Frontier* (New York: Doubleday, 1991).

9. Lawrence Frank, Martin Andresen and Thomas Schmid, "Obesity Relationships with Community Design, Physical Activity, and Time Spent in Cars," *American Journal of Preventive Medicine* 27, 2 (August 2004), 87–96.

10. Robert Bruegmann, *Sprawl: A Compact History* (Chicago: University of Chicago Press, 2005), 56.

11. James Howard Kunstler, *Home from Nowhere: Remaking our Everyday World for the 21st Century* (New York: Simon and Schuster, 1996), 17.

Chapter 4 **Environment and Energy**

1. www.epa.gov/heatisland/.

2. David Urbinato, "London's Historic Pea-Soupers," *EPA Journal*, 1994. www.epa.gov/history/topics/perspect/london.htm.

3. In the fourteenth century, between a quarter and two-thirds of the population of Europe and western Asia were killed by the pandemic known as the Black Plague, which was spread by fleas and rats. Such epidemics re-emerged frequently in the filth of large cities like London in the mid-seventeenth century and in China, Asia and Russia in the 1850s. http://en.wikipedia.org/wiki/Bubonic_plague.

4. John Lorinc, "The City Builder," *Spacing*, Winter 2006.

5. Jon Gertner, "The Perfect Drought: Will Population Growth and Climate Change Leave the West without Water?" *The New York Times Magazine*, October 21, 2007, 68–77, 104, 154–155.

6. George Packer, "The Megacity: Decoding the Chaos of Lagos," *The New Yorker*, November 13, 2006, 62–75.

7. UN Habitat, *The State of the World's Cities Report 2006-2007* (London: Earthscan, 2006), 74.

8. *Meeting the MDG Drinking Water and Sanitation Target: The Urban and Rural Challenge of the Decade*. World Health Organization and UNICEF, 2006, 18.

9. Frances Williams, "Health Risk of Air Pollution Is Global Burden, Says WHO," *Financial Times* of London, October 6, 2006.

10. Packer, "The Megacity," 74.

11. Matthew Power, "The Magic Mountain: Trickle-Down Economics in a Philippine Dump." *Harper's*, December 2006, 57–68.

12. UN Habitat, *The State of the World's Cities*, 74.

13. David Owen, "Green Manhattan," *The New Yorker*, October 18, 2004.

14. William Little, "The Future Must Float," *Financial Times* of London, January 20, 2007.

15. www.msnbc.msn.com/id/11281267.

16. Zakir Hussain, "Government Preparing for Possibility of Rising Sea Levels," *The Straits Times*, April 23, 2007.

17. Little, "The Future Must Float."

18. Canadian Plastics Industry Association, http://www.plastics.ca/newsroom/default.php?ID=162.

19. California Integrated Waste Management Board, www.ciwmb.ca.gov/Tires/Products/.

20. Federal Highway Administration, www.fhwa.dot.gov/pavement/recycling/rcaca.cfm.

21. Christopher Heredia, "Ordinance Seeks Ban on Plastic Bags," *San Francisco Chronicle*, May 11, 2007, B6.

22. www.dti.gov.uk/innovation/sustainability/packaging/page29072.html.

23. http://europa.eu/scadplus/leg/en/lvb/l21210.htm.

24. www.nysunworks.com.

25. UN Habitat, *The State of the World's Cities*, 107.

26. Ibid.

27. www.greenroofs.net/index.php?option=com_content&task=view&id=555&Itemid=115.

28. Patrick O'Neill, "PSU Taking Wind Power for a Whirl," *The Oregonian*, April 26, 2007.

29. European Photovoltaic Industry Association/Greenpeace, "Solar Generation: Solar Electricity for Over One Billion People and Two Million Jobs by 2020," 6, www.epia.org/documents/SG3.pdf.

30. Mark Clayton, "Solar Power Hits Suburbia," *Christian Science Monitor*, February 12, 2004, www.csmonitor.com/2004/0212/p14s02-sten.html.

31. http://edition.cnn.com/2007/WORLD/asiapcf/11/12/eco.about.csp/index.html.

32. Nicolai Ouroussoff, "Why Are They Greener Than We Are?" *New York Times Magazine*, May 20, 2007, 62-66.

Chapter 5 **Cities and Transportation**

1. US Department of Transportation statistics, www.dot.gov/affairs/dot5307.htm.

2. The gun-related death figure is for 2004. The Brady Campaign, www.bradycampaign.org/facts/factsheets/pdf/firearm_facts.pdf.

3. Municipal Fund, International Finance Corporation (World Bank Group), "Urban Transport Strategy Review," Chapter 6: The Urban Road System, www.ifc.org/ifcext/municipalfund.nsf/Content/Urban_Transport.

4. Canadian and US Censuses, 2000, 2001, as cited in Jack Jedwab, "Getting to Work in North America's Major Cities and Dependence on Cars" (Montreal: Association for Canadan Studies, 2004).

5. Andrew Heisz and Sebastien LaRochelle-Côté, "Work and Commuting in Census Metropolitan Areas, 1996 to 2001" (Statistics Canada, catalogue 89-613, no. 007, June 1, 2005), 52.

6. Transit serves many categories of users – students, the elderly, commuters.

But transit ridership levels tend to rise and fall with the economy because when people are laid off, they don't need to take transit to work.

7. International Union of Railways, www.uic.asso.fr/gv/article.php3?id_article=22.

8. California High Speed Rail, www.cahighspeedrail.ca.gov/whats_new/.

9. Jeffrey Tumlin and Adam Millard-Ball (2006), "Parking for Transit-Oriented Development, ITE Annual Meeting" (www.ite.org). Cited at www.vtpi.org/tdm/tdm45.htm.

10. Glen Johnson, "Governor Seeks to Take Control of Big Dig Inspections," *Boston Globe*, July 13, 2006. See also www.massturnpike.com/bigdig/index.html.

11. The Westway Development Trust, www.westway.org/.

12. Report of the Committee for the International Symposium on Road Pricing, "International Perspectives on Road Pricing" (Washington DC: Transportation Research Board of the National Academies, 2003), 29, www.trb.org.

13. Wikipedia, http://en.wikipedia.org/wiki/Stockholm_congestion_tax.

14. El Consorcio Regional de Transportes de Madrid, "La Introgracio del sistema de transportes en Comunidad de Madrid" (Proceedings Volume: 55th Congreso de la UITP, May 4-9, 2003).

15. Wikipedia, http://en.wikipedia.org/wiki/Table_of_Bus_Rapid_Transit_Systems_in_North_America.

16. http://itdp.org/STe/ste23/guangzhou.html.

17. http://itdp.org/STe/ste23/johannesburg.html.

18. Clyde Haberman, "Koch Says He's Prepared to Get Rid of Bike Paths," *New York Times*, June 30, 1981.

19. Michael Moore, "Ottawa Bike Routes Axed in Budget," *Globe and Mail*, April 29, 1981.

20. Katrin Bennhold, *International Herald Tribune*, July 15, 2007. www.iht.com/articles/2007/07/15/news/paris.php.

21. Michelle Lalonde, "Bogotá is Poor, Crowded, But Sets a Good Example," Montreal *Gazette*, September 24, 2003.

Chapter 6 **Urban Poverty**

1. Robert Neuwirth, *Shadow Cities: A Billion Squatters, A New Urban World* (New York: Routledge/Taylor and Francis Group, 2005), xiii.

2. Eric Mann, *Los Angeles Times*, June 26, 1988.

3. For further information, see the Service Employees International Union's website, www.sieu.org/property/janitors.

4. John Lorinc, "Union Maid," *Report on Business* Magazine, May 2006.

5. http://cml.upenn.edu/redlining/intro.html. A website with information about redlining in Philadelphia, maintained by Amy Hillier, a lecturer with the Urban Studies Program of the University of Pennsylvania.

6. Department for Communities and Local Government, "Homes for the Future: More Affordable, More Sustainable" (London, The Stationary Office, July 2007). The full report is available at www.communities.gov.uk/documents/housing/pdf/439986.

7. UN Habitat, *The State of the World's Cities*, vii–ix.

8. Ibid., 12.

9. Timothy Garton Ash, "Where Democracy Is Mocked by Poverty," *Globe and Mail*, July 3, 2007, A15.

10. Davis, *Planet of Slums*, 13.

11. Ash, "Where Democracy Is Mocked by Poverty."

12. *Meeting the MDG Drinking Water and Sanitation Target,* 14–15.

13. Davis, *Planet of Slums*, 145–46.

14. Neuwirth, *Shadow Cities*, 103.

15. Davis, *Planet of Slums*, 139.

16. UN Habitat, *The State of the World's Cities*, 82.

17. Marcus Gee, "Squalor or Opportunity?" *Globe and Mail*, June 25, 2007.

18. Neuwirth, *Shadow Cities*, 8.

19. Rualdo Menegat, "Participatory Democracy in Porto Alegre, Brazil" (International Institute for Environment and Development, 2002), www.iied.org/NR/agbioliv/pla_notes/documents/plan_04402.pdf.

20. Neuwirth, *Shadow Cities*, 142.

Chapter 7 Crime, Epidemics and Terrorism

1. Kotkin, *The City*, 154.

2. UN Habitat, *The State of the World's Cities*, 142.

3. Malcolm Gladwell, "The Tipping Point," *The New Yorker*, June 3, 1996, www.gladwell.com/1996/1996_06_03_a_tipping.htm.

4. Australian Institute of Criminology, www.aic.gov.au/publications/cfi/cfi120.html.

5. www.statcan.ca/Daily/English/080220/d080220b.htm.

6. William Langewiesche, "City of Fear," *Vanity Fair*, April 2007, 158.

7. The United Nations Office of Drugs and Crime in 2007 reported that Canada has the highest rate of marijuana use in the developed world. Indeed, according to unofficial estimates, pot has become British

Columbia's second-largest export crop, after wood products.

8. Insite, as Vancouver's safe injection facility is known, is being closely monitored by addiction researchers. The results can be found at www.vch.ca/sis/research.htm.

9. Michael Bliss, *Plague: A Story of Smallpox in Montreal* (Toronto, McClelland and Stewart, 1991), 25.

10. A brief online history of the 1918–19 flu is available at http://virus.stanford.edu/uda/.

11. UN Habitat, *The State of the World's Cities*, 115.

12. Ibid., 116.

13. www.commondreams.org/headlines05/0830-02.htm.

14. Civil libertarians have had little success in slowing the deployment of such security systems. Law enforcement officials say that the number of cameras makes it nearly impossible for the police to use these surveillance devices to monitor public behavior; rather, the cameras serve as a deterrent and assist investigators in identifying suspects in crimes committed in public spaces.

15. Scott Bollens, "Ethnic Stability and Urban Reconstruction: Policy Dilemmas in Polarized Cities," in *The Urban Politics Reader*, Elizabeth A. Strom and John H. Mollenkopf, eds. (New York: Routledge, 2007), 257–59.

16. Ibid., 260–61.

17. Stephanie Nolen, "The Fall and Rise of a Johannesburg Icon," *Globe and Mail*, July 30, 2007.

18. Ibid.

For Further Information

Ascher, Kate. *The Works: Anatomy of a City*. New York: The Penguin Press, 2005.

Baxandall, Rosalyn and Elizabeth Ewen. *Picture Windows: How the Suburbs Happened*. New York: Basic Books, 2000.

Bliss, Michael. *Plague: A Story of Smallpox in Montreal*. Toronto: HarperCollins, 1991.

Brenner, Neil and Roger Keil. *The Global Cities Reader*. London and New York: Routledge, 2006.

Bruegmann, Robert. *Sprawl: A Compact History*. Chicago: University of Chicago Press, 2005.

Calvino, Italo. *Invisible Cities*. Translated from Italian by William Weaver. London: Vintage, 1997.

Davis, Mike. *City of Quartz: Excavating the Future in Los Angeles*. New York: Vintage Books, 1992.

Davis, Mike. *Planet of Slums*. London and New York: Verso, 2006.

Eaton, Ruth. *Ideal Cities: Utopianism and the (Un)Built Environment*. London and New York: Thames and Hudson, 2002.

Florida, Richard. *The Rise of the Creative Class…and How It's Transforming Work, Leisure, Community, and Everyday Life*. New York: Basic Books, 2002.

Garreau, Joel. *Edge City: Life on the New Frontier*. New York: Doubleday, 1991.

Hall, Sir Peter. *Cities in Civilization*. London: Weidenfeld and Nicholson, 1998.

Jacobs, Jane. *The Death and Life of Great American Cities*. New York and Toronto: Alfred Knopf/Random House, 1961.

Kingwell, Mark. *Concrete Reveries: Consciousness and the City*. Toronto: Viking Canada, 2008.

Kunstler, James Howard. *The Geography of Nowhere: The Rise and Decline of America's Man-Made Landscapes*. New York: Simon and Schuster, 1996.

Kostof, Spiro. *The City Shaped: Urban Patterns and Meanings Through History*. London: Thames and Hudson, 1991.

Kotkin, Joel. *The City: A Global History*. New York: Random House, 2005.

LeGates, Richard and Frederic Stout, eds. *The City Reader*. London and New York: Routledge, 1996.

Lorinc, John. *The New City: How the Crisis in Canada's Urban Centres Is Re-shaping the Nation*. Toronto: Penguin, 2006.

Mumford, Lewis. *The City in History*. New York: Harcourt, 1961.

Neuwirth, Robert. *Shadow Cities: A Billion Squatters*, A New Urban World. New York and London: Routledge, 2006.

Rybczynski, Witold. *City Life: Urban Expectations in a New World*. Toronto, HarperCollins, 1995.

Sewell, John. *The Shape of the City: Toronto Struggles with Modern Planning*. Toronto: University of Toronto Press, 1993.

Tung, Anthony. *Preserving the World's Great Cities: The Destruction and Renewal of the Historic Metropolis*. New York: Three Rivers Press, 2001.

White, E.B. *Here Is New York*. New York: New York Review of Books, 2000.

Wilkinson, Richard. *Unhealthy Societies: The Afflictions of Inequality*. London: Routledge, 1996.

Acknowledgments

I must thank Patsy Aldana for her persistence in persuading me to write this book after I pitched it to her over lunch one day and then promptly got cold feet. It was a wonderful project to do and I'm grateful she didn't give up. Jane Springer did a terrific job editing the manuscript.

I am lucky to be part of a wide circle of relatives, friends, neighbors and colleagues who have provided me with great support and companionship. And to Victoria, Jacob and Sammy: all my love.

Groundwood Books would like to thank Ariel Baker-Gibbs for proofreading, Leon Grek for drawing the chart, Deborah Viets for copyediting, and Gillian Watts for the index.

Index